LOVING
PEOPLE

LOVING PEOPLE

DR. JOHN TOWNSEND

THOMAS NELSON
Since 1798

NASHVILLE DALLAS MEXICO CITY RIO DE JANEIRO BEIJING

Loving People
© 2007 by Dr. John Townsend

Published in Nashville, Tennessee, by Thomas Nelson. Thomas Nelson is a registered trademark of Thomas Nelson, Inc.

Published in association with Yates & Yates, LLP, 1100 Town & Country Road, Suite 1300, Orange, CA 92868.

Thomas Nelson, Inc. titles may be purchased in bulk for educational, business, fund-raising, or sales promotional use. For information, please e-mail SpecialMarkets@ThomasNelson.com.

All Scripture quotations, unless otherwise indicated, are taken from the *Holy Bible*, New Living Translation, © 1996. Used by permission of Tyndale House Publishers, Inc., Wheaton, Illinois 60189. All rights reserved.

Scripture quotations marked NIV are taken from the HOLY BIBLE, NEW INTERNATIONAL VERSION®. © 1973, 1978, 1984, International Bible Society. Used by permission of Zondervan Bible Publishing House. All rights reserved.

Scripture quotations noted NASB are taken from the NEW AMERICAN STANDARD BIBLE®, © 1960, 1962, 1963, 1968, 1971, 1972, 1973, 1975, 1977, 1995 by the Lockman Foundation. Used by permission.

Some identifying names and details have been changed to protect the identities of those involved.

Library of Congress Cataloging-in-Publication Data

Townsend, John Sims, 1952-
    Loving people / John Townsend.
      p. cm.
    Includes bibliographical references.
    ISBN 978-0-8499-1961-9 (hardcover)
    ISBN 978-0-7852-8952-4 (IE)
    1. Love--Religious aspects—Christianity. 2. Interpersonal relations—Religious aspects—Christianity. I. Title.
BV4639.T67 2007
248.4--dc22

                  2007041997

Printed in the United States of America

07 08 09 10 11 RRD 9 8 7 6 5 4 3 2 1

To all who desire the good
that comes from loving and being loved.
May God bless you.

CONTENTS

ACKNOWLEDGMENTS

I would like to thank the following people who helped bring this book about:

Sealy Yates and Jeana Ledbetter, my literary agents: You have shepherded this book, as you have so many others, into its present form. You are unique in your care and guidance of what books and their importance are all about.

Mike Hyatt, president and CEO, Thomas Nelson Publishers: Your ability to keep both the big picture and the individual relationship in mind is a great encouragement to me. You are much appreciated.

Byron Williamson: Thanks for your creativity and vision in coming up with the concept and bringing it to me. I appreciate all the warmth and ideas you bring to the literary world.

Joey Paul: Your craftsmanship and instincts helped form the direction of this material. Thanks for the support and direction.

Jennifer Stair: You bring a great ability to being the advocate for the reader in your editorial competence. The book is better because of your work.

The staff of Cloud-Townsend Resources—Maureen Price, Janet Williams, Jodi Coker, Debra Nili, Patti Schenkel, and Bonnie Winslow: thanks for the hours of hard work and making it all fun at the same time.

Dr. Keith Edwards and Dr. Tom Okamoto: Thanks for your valuable insights into the current research aspects of love and connection. You bring clarity and weight to the material.

Dr. Jay Martin: Thanks for your coaching and direction throughout the writing process. Your ability to be both deeply conceptual and totally practical has been an incredible help.

ACKNOWLEDGMENTS

The CCN Solutions by Satellite attendees: thanks for engaging with the material that formed this book and being together with me in the growth process.

Dr. Henry Cloud: I am grateful for the many years of being a partner and friend in studying and experiencing the concepts in this book. Thanks for being there!

PART 1

What Is Love?

O N E

Learning to Love

"I love you."

These three words can change your life. Whether you are on the giving or receiving end of these words, they reach deeply into us and transform us. They remind us that love is one of the most important aspects of our lives, guiding our steps from our early years to our last days.

Let me introduce this subject with a couple of examples of the impact of love, one from the perspective of youth and another from that of old age. First, I recently took my wife and kids on a ski vacation during a school break. When it was time to return home, one of our sons wanted to stay longer to snowboard with friends. Austin, one of his best friends, was among them. We made arrangements for other parents to drive him home later that day, and my wife and I left with our other son.

That evening, our son called us and said that everything was a big mess. He misjudged his time and took off for one more ride down the mountain when it would have been better to meet the others who were driving him home. On top of that, he accidentally fell into a deep snowbank and had difficulty getting himself out. It was a frightening experience for him.

By the time he got back to the pickup spot, he had made the entire party late starting on the long ride home. Naturally, the others were frustrated and angry with him. It was an unpleasant experience for everyone in the car.

When our son got home, we talked about what happened. He said, "Dad,

I know I was wrong about taking the extra ride. It was my fault that we were all so late. I shouldn't have done it. Everyone was right to be mad at me."

Then he added, "But what I remember most is what Austin said. While everyone was yelling at me, all Austin said was, 'Are you all right?' He was worried about me in that snowbank."

> HOW WE OPERATE AS LOVING PEOPLE, AND WHO WE LOVE, WILL MAKE A GREAT DIFFERENCE IN THE COURSES OF OUR LIVES.

Certainly there is no question that my son needed to learn a lesson about responsibility and judgment, and I think he did. But what mattered even more was Austin's concern for him. That is because love comes first.

Then, in a fast-forward to the other end of the life span, I also recently attended the funeral of Howard, a friend of mine who died in his eighties. Howard's memorial service was a time of grief, but it was also a celebration because it was all about love, for that was a large part of Howard's life. People were invited to say something about Howard and their relationship with him. Here are a few things that were shared:

"He cared about me."
"He loved people without judgment."
"You knew Howard really was there for you."
"He drew people to him."
"He changed my life for the better."

Over and over again, Howard's friends and family spoke about how he made them feel, how he connected with them, and how he brought life to them through his words and his actions.

How we operate as loving people, and who we love, will make a great difference in the courses of our lives. You can probably remember right now an experience in which someone affected you a great deal by either how much, how helpfully, or even how poorly he or she loved you. These events and people stay with us, for good or for bad, forever. They get inside—and they stay inside. Love matters to us.

THE MOST IMPORTANT PART OF LIFE

Love is our highest endeavor. Our lives are evaluated by how much—or how little—we love. Our quality of life and even the number of our days are affected by love. In fact, it is only to the extent that we love well and deeply that we are truly alive.

Can you recall a time that you experienced genuine love? Chances are, you have at least one experience of love seared deeply into your memory. That's because we assign landmark status to the times we have experienced love. We vividly remember these people and events forever. We use them as reference points and standards by which we compare our present relationships. The converse is also true: we never forget the pain of love lost, love gone bad, or the absence of love.

> LOVE IS OUR HIGHEST ENDEAVOR.

Certainly there are many things that give meaning and significance to our lives, such as our work, activities, and passions. And all of these are highly important and valuable. But without love motivating, driving, guiding them, they are empty. As the apostle Paul points out, "If I could speak all the languages of earth and of angels, but didn't love others, I would only be a noisy gong or a clanging cymbal."[1]

PEOPLE WHO LOVE OTHERS, AND WHAT THEY RECEIVE

How does all this relate to you today? You are probably reading this book because you are interested in becoming a more loving person, and my intent is to help you do that. In this book, I will share principles and skills to enable you to become a person who truly cares for others. Learning to love others authentically, and in ways that matter to them, is one of the best things anyone can do. Loving people will not only be beneficial to others, but your life will also change for the better.

No matter what the results, most people don't regret the time and effort they spent in loving, if only for what they have learned and with whom they have connected. However, many people do regret the time they avoided learning to love. You don't want to look back on your life and realize you missed out on love. You need to be busy today in loving people so you can be able to reflect on how meaningful and good your life has been because of your willingness and commitment to love.

Now, the rightness and helpfulness of love does not mean pain is not involved. In fact, sometimes when we do something caring, we can get hurt.

LEARNING TO LOVE OTHERS AUTHENTICALLY, AND IN WAYS THAT MATTER TO THEM, IS ONE OF THE BEST THINGS ANYONE CAN DO.

For example, have you ever opened up to someone emotionally and then had things go wrong for you? Most of us have. Even so, in the long run, love is very much worth the pain. As C. S. Lewis notes in his book *The Four Loves*, "The only place outside of Heaven where you can be perfectly safe from all the dangers and perturbations of love is Hell."[2]

You may have noticed that the title of this book has a double meaning. *Loving* can be both a verb (the action of demonstrating love) and an adjective (the description of someone who demonstrates love). The intent here is to bring attention to the reality that both meanings are necessary for each other to exist. If you want to be a loving person, you must actively show love to people. And if you want to love people, you are to be a person characterized by loving.

People want to learn to love for different reasons. Some want to improve a specific relationship, such as with a spouse, child, or friend. Others would like to see love affect other aspects of life. And others want to have improved connections in general.

Here are some of the benefits of becoming the loving person you were designed to become:

- *Better relationships.* The more you learn to love, the more improvement you experience in relationships that matter to you. You will have healthier relationships, and you will become better connected to your friends and loved ones.

- *The experience of love.* Love can involve a truly wonderful experience that makes hard times and suffering worthwhile. In and of itself, love fills us up and makes us glad to be alive, even when it hurts.

- *The capacity for intimacy.* Intimacy is an important aspect of love. As you become more loving, you are able to open yourself up to people in a deep way and to be connected to the hearts of others.

- *Freedom.* People who learn to love are out of jail—that is, they are free from the prisons of fear, guilt, and pretending to be someone they are not. They make their own choices and decisions. They tell the truth without being afraid. They can be vulnerable with the right people.

- *Joy and happiness.* Love brings a positive outlook and contentment to life. When you are a loving person, you end up receiving much more than you give.

- *Success in goals and dreams.* Loving people create for themselves a foundation of safety and encouragement that helps launch them into achieving their dreams, vision, and goals.

- *Personal growth and healing.* People who love can get the resources they need from others so they can make the changes and transformations that will help them grow. Love is essential to any personal growth efforts.

- *Leadership abilities.* The best leaders are those who can connect in positive ways to people in their organizations—inspiring, motivating, and guiding them to excellence.

- *Good effects on others.* When you love, others are helped. Loving people encourage, support, empathize with, and confront those in their lives, and the result is that they are the better for it. You can see transformation in the lives of others in whom you have invested love. Nobody changes permanently without love; therefore loving people provides the foundation for others to grow.

- *Quality of life.* People who love and are loved tend to have a better life experience all around. Some researchers believe that loving people have better physical and emotional health, and even longer lives because of the positive effects of love.

- *Spiritual growth.* Love was created and designed by God, and it is his greatest gift to us. Love is the deepest part of God's nature. As we learn the principles of love, we also become closer to God, who teaches and models the experience for us to have with one another: "Just as I have loved you, you should love each other."[3] A life filled with loving people, and loving the One who made people, is a worthwhile life.

WE ARE LOOKING FOR LOVE

At the end of the day—more accurately, at the end of our lives—we all want to experience and give love more than anything else. Success, pleasurable activities, material possessions, even a noble purpose in life all pale beside our longing for love. The pages of history are filled with people who have gladly given up treasures and opportunities for the understanding and experience of love.

We want to know the mystery and power of love, to receive it inside our hearts, and ultimately to give it to others. The people whom we most admire and want to emulate are often those who are most familiar with and the best bestowers of love. Those who are the most loving are also those who have received, and made good use of, the love they have experienced.

Most of us can recall a time we have experienced true love. Maybe a special time in our marriage or a memorable romance. Or a late-night conversation with a friend. Or a warm family experience. Or a grandmother's smile. But the point is, for most of us, the spark of love still exists somewhere within us; it has not gone out. It may be undeveloped and frail, and we may not know how to fan the flames of love again, but it is there.

Love is not always foremost on our minds. We may forget about it for a while or avoid it for some reason. We may get involved in our work, our activities, our childrearing, or some mission in life to the extent that it temporarily leaves our awareness. Or, if love has gone bad for us, we may simply deny that love is important. This helps keep the pain away for a while.

Sooner or later, however, we find ourselves in a situation in which we feel safe and know it's OK to be honest. It may be when we are alone in a quiet place. Or with a companion who helps us look into ourselves. Or in prayer. Or after one of life's various failures or losses, when we can no longer pretend about our feelings. It is during these times that we regain contact with the reality that we want, desire, and need love—*real* love—in some form. And we also want to give love to those we care about. Experiencing and giving love are signs of life to us—that we are here, that God is real, and that our lives matter.

> EXPERIENCING AND GIVING LOVE ARE SIGNS OF LIFE TO US— THAT WE ARE HERE, THAT GOD IS REAL, AND THAT OUR LIVES MATTER.

CARING ISN'T ENOUGH

I have become increasingly aware of a significant problem in the area of love and relationships—*caring isn't enough.* Care and love aren't the same thing.

Almost any of us could say that we truly care about some people. We can freely admit that, and we are glad these people are in our lives. We want what's best for them. But the reality is often that *we don't know how to treat those we care about in the most loving way.* We want to be the best for those people, but we don't know how to love them in the way that is best. That is, we would like to be close to them, to be a positive influence for them, and to bring them to intimacy and a better life. But there is a disconnect between our care for those we love and how we address or approach them. Let me illustrate this point with several examples.

THE HUSBAND WHO CAN'T BE CLOSE

Christine and Jeff are a married couple who are friends of mine. One day Christine called me and wanted some pointers for her relationship with Jeff.

She said, "I know he loves me and the kids; I have no questions about that. Jeff would do anything for us. But when he and I are together, I don't feel it inside. Nothing really happens between us.

> **THE REALITY IS OFTEN THAT WE DON'T KNOW HOW TO TREAT THOSE WE CARE ABOUT IN THE MOST LOVING WAY.**

"We'll talk about the day and the kids, and then it gets quiet. I'll ask him all sorts of questions about his reactions to his work and his stresses, and he'll tell me a little and stop. If I don't ask more, he'll look at the TV or get on the Web. Then we go to sleep."

I said, "So even though you know he loves you, you don't experience it."

"Yes," Christine said. "Sometimes I get upset and tell him that the relationship is lonely, and I want more from him. But this doesn't help. In fact, it seems to distance him further. He'll say, 'I'm sorry,' or 'I'll be praying for you,' but I think he is just afraid and doesn't know what to do. He is just trying to say anything to keep me from being mad at him. And then he shuts down even more. He's not mad or mean to me. He's just . . . in the room."

Now think about this scenario from Jeff's point of view. He most likely felt terrible that the love he had for Christine was not getting to her where she needed it. The caring wasn't enough.

THE WOMAN WHO CAN'T CONFRONT HER MOM

Susan is a working single mom whose own mother, Marilyn, drives her crazy. Marilyn is a nice person and genuinely cares about Susan, but she can be quite dependent and self-centered without being aware of it. She needs a lot from her daughter, which can be pretty draining for Susan.

Susan told me, "Most of our conversations end up being about how difficult Dad is, and her life and stresses. I listen a lot because I know she needs a friend. But when I try to bring up how things are going for me, she'll somehow turn things back to herself. Like last week when I told her that my son was misbehaving at school and how hard that is with me working full-time, she said, 'At least you have your youth and energy going for you. Think how it is at my age, having to deal with your father's problems.' I had no idea what to say to that, so

I gave up. I feel bad, because she doesn't have a lot of friends, and that's probably why. But I have no idea how to say whatever will help. So I listen."

Susan loves her mom, but the listening isn't enough. Marilyn has a problem with relating that affects her life, her connection with her daughter, and most likely her own marriage. Susan needs a way to truly and effectively love her mom in a way that would provide answers and make a difference. That help would be in the form of some sort of a confrontive conversation. But Susan has no idea where to start. Not only that, but she doesn't want to hurt or injure her mom.

THE MAN WHO DOESN'T KNOW HOW TO HELP HIS DEPRESSED FRIEND

Miguel, a businessman I know, has a friend at work named Phil. Their families have done some social things, and Miguel and Phil have gone to some games together. They have a pretty good relationship. However, during a watercooler conversation, Phil told Miguel that he was dealing with depression and that it was affecting his job and his marriage. Miguel didn't know what to do to help and called me for advice.

He said, "This isn't my area of expertise. I am totally out of my comfort zone. I want to help, and I don't want to make things worse for Phil. I can see that he is really struggling. I told Phil I'd pray for him and that he can call anytime. But honestly, I have no idea what I should do if he calls and needs help. I kind of hope he doesn't, but it feels mean to even be thinking that." I am sure Miguel is a good friend. But his care for Phil doesn't help Phil's struggle. In fact, Miguel's lack of ability to help Phil even has him thinking about distancing from his friend.

LOVE IS MUCH MORE THAN GOOD INTENTIONS

The list could go on, but the pattern is consistent. Most people I know want their love to help, to matter, and to change things. But their positive feelings and concern don't accomplish what needs to be done. The old saying that "the road to hell is paved with good intentions" is too harsh for this situation. It might more accurately be said, for someone who wants to be a more loving person, that "the road paved with good intentions goes nowhere." Love is much more than good feelings or intentions. It has direction, movement, and purpose.

But *while we may feel love, we may not be doing love.* Most of us don't know how to experience and become competent in the art form of love. We may value it and desire it. We may even attempt to elicit love from others. But we don't have a lot of knowledge about how to create and develop love.

Some of us are reasonably happy with the quality of loving relationships we are in but would like to have more, to see that capacity grow. Others of us see that we aren't close to what we would like to experience and want a lot more love coming our way. And others are hesitant about receiving and showing love, because they have been hurt by someone in the past.

> **WHILE WE MAY FEEL LOVE, WE MAY NOT BE DOING LOVE.**

Regardless of where you are in your desire to experience love, if you're like most people, you probably don't think you have any control over how to make it happen. Many of us have the same view of love that we have when we happen upon a brilliant sunset: We are awestruck. We enjoy it and take it in. We mention it to our friends at dinner. We may even return to the same site the next day, hoping it will happen again. Sometimes it does, sometimes it doesn't.

Similarly, many of us simply hope that love will happen, that it will show up and find us. We seek out people with whom we want to experience love. We wait patiently for it to come. And sometimes it does, sometimes it doesn't.

Even people whose lives bear the fruit of decades of loving and being loved don't often tell us how to do this. Take the love of a good marriage, for example. Ask a dozen couples who have been happily married for many years what their secret is, and you're likely to get a dozen answers: "Caring about the other's feelings." "Mutual interests." "Honesty." "Family." "God and church." "A sense of humor." My experience is that most of these individuals are able to do love, and do it well. But they aren't as able to articulate the mechanics of love.

LOVE CAN BE LEARNED

Sometimes people think that love, and the capacity to truly love others, is not meant for them. *Some people just have a natural gift for it*, they think. Others may think, *Loving others is too much work, and I don't want to take the risk.* And still others may think, *I've had some damage in my relationships, and it's not worth it anymore.*

All these thoughts have their share of truth. Some people do have an innate ability to love, and some people do get beat up by bad relationships. But no matter what your previous experience in loving others, you can develop the capacity to be a loving person. And that is the purpose of this book. In these pages I will show you specific principles you can learn and steps you can take to experience love in your relationships and to give it to others.

You were designed for love; that is part of the human architecture. This material is not about becoming someone you're not. In fact, it is about becoming more of who you were truly meant to be. It is ultimately about the authentic part of you that God created. It may be buried way down inside, inaccessible, frozen, dormant, or undeveloped. But you have a God-given capacity to give and receive love, and you will be a better person when it begins to emerge and become part of your everyday life. There are specific skills you can learn in order to "do" love, no matter what your background.

NO MATTER WHAT YOUR PREVIOUS EXPERIENCE IN LOVING OTHERS, YOU CAN DEVELOP THE CAPACITY TO BE A LOVING PERSON.

At this point, you may have an objection like this: *Love isn't a "how-to." That sounds artificial and forced. I can't make myself feel and experience love by some act of the will.*

This makes sense. We cannot force ourselves to feel anything. Feelings are the result of changes inside us. They aren't a cause; they are an effect. Trying to will ourselves to feel love doesn't work. Yet when we say that love is only a feeling, we reduce it to something less than what it truly is. As I said earlier, love encompasses and experiences feelings, but love is not limited to feelings. It is much more—genuine love involves the heart, soul, and mind. We can all learn to develop this ability and enjoy the lasting and abundant benefits of love.

Of course, learning to love is not effortless; there is work and diligence involved. As the saying goes, you get what you pay for. Basically, there are two criteria for those who want to be loving people—humility and tolerating discomfort. Humility refers to accepting the fact that you do not know it all already. And tolerating discomfort is about being willing to try new things and take risks, some of which will involve vulnerability and failure. Those two requirements will stand you in good stead in becoming a loving person.

Here is a way to understand how taking steps and learning skills can help you become a loving person. Think about the last time you rented a movie to watch at home. If your experience is anything like it is at my house, it can be quite a project, requiring lots of steps. You drive to the store, select and pay for the movie, buy the popcorn, drive home, microwave your popcorn and fix drinks, turn off all the lights (even the little light showing through the crack under the bathroom door), forget your real life, suspend your disbelief, enter the director's world, identify with the characters, feel what they are feeling, and experience drama, excitement, surprise, fear, horror, love, insight, or humor. When you think about it, you're doing a lot of work. But the end result is, depending on the quality of the movie, an experience that becomes part of you. Who can't recall quotes and scenes from their favorite movies?

> LOVE MAY BE A MYSTERY, BUT IF YOU FOLLOW THESE PRACTICAL STEPS, YOU CAN DEVELOP SOME MASTERY TO ITS PRESENCE IN YOUR LIFE.

In the same way, the steps you take in this book will help you enter into experiences that will change, develop, and increase your ability to be loved and to love others. Love may be a mystery, but if you follow these practical steps, you can develop some mastery to its presence in your life.

The ideas and steps I share in this book come from a variety of sources. My formal training in psychology and theology involved a great deal of study in the nature of personal relationships. As a clinical psychologist, I have worked over the years with many clients in various settings, and my interactions and observations have helped me to compile the commonalities of love's importance, healing power, and development. In my consultations with leaders and organizations, I have learned how love affects people in the workplace. In speaking in conferences and on the radio, I have had contact with thousands of people who, though they may begin with a problem, ultimately find a solution in love.

In addition to my professional experience, my own life has also been touched by some profoundly significant people who have modeled love and taught me how to seek the best for others. I have seen firsthand the incredible power of love, and I have witnessed transformations in many, many people who thought they could never experience or give love. By walking through the steps in this book, their lives have been changed from seeing love as unattainable or perhaps optional, to making love a central part of their everyday lives. All this is to say that becoming a loving person, or a more loving person, is within the reach of anyone who truly desires to do so.

THE KEY ASPECTS OF LOVE

To help you take the necessary steps to becoming a loving person, I have organized this book into the key aspects of what caring is all about. Each of these aspects helps in becoming a fully loving person:

- *Connecting*—making an emotional bond

- *Truth-Telling*—honesty that serves the other person

- *Healing*—repairing brokenness

- *Letting Go*—giving up what should be surrendered

- *Romancing*—the unique love of being a couple

You may find yourself gravitating to some of these aspects and not to others. You may have a natural gift in one or more of these. No one is an expert in all of these areas, but all five of these key aspects of love have value. The best approach is to understand how each one fits in the big picture and then to work on the ones you need the most work on.

The skill-building part of love will be prominent in these sections. As I describe each aspect, I will also show how you can create, grow, and direct love in this area so that you can gain experience, success, and confidence in your ability to become a loving person. The stories and illustrations in these chapters will serve to flesh out these ideas and to connect you emotionally to the concepts.

THINKING IN TERMS OF RELATIONSHIP

As you read this book, keep in mind the people you care about and want to be able to love better and more fully. People who care about you. People in your past whom you want to be more like. People who may be very difficult to love. Keep these individuals, and their attributes, in your awareness. It will help you make more sense and use out of the material. Developing and accessing love is relational; it can't be done alone. Learning about love can't be done out of the context of relationship, as you might be able to do with taking an online course or learning a trade. Unlike a self-help course that can be taken in the privacy of your living room, you can't develop the art of love without interacting with other people.

So be assured that *you can learn to be a loving person*, whether you want to go from good to great, clueless to connected, or damaged to healed. It doesn't matter where you start; it is most important just to start. Love will show you the next step.

In the next chapter I will begin with a working definition of *love* so you will not get lost in the many ways the word is used. You will also learn what the nature of love is all about.

TWO

The Nature of Love

Imagine that Jay Leno is doing a man-on-the-street interview with you. He asks, "What is love?" What would you say? Closeness? Romance? Concern? How God feels toward us?

We all have some sort of intuitive understanding of love, because love is a significant part of the human experience. But it is likely that most of us have not thought through a formal definition of what love actually is. Since we are dealing with one of life's most important experiences, it is helpful to define *love* in a way that is accurate and useful.

WHAT IS LOVE?

To understand what being a loving person is, we need to understand the nature of love, and that is a large project. Philosophers and theologians have debated the question "What is love?" for centuries. Countless books have been written on the subject. *Love* is one of the most used, most cherished, and most misunderstood words in human history. It has been used to describe a relationship, a feeling, a passion, an action, a philosophy, a lifestyle, and more.

WHAT DOES THE BIBLE SAY ABOUT LOVE?
The Bible uses several different Hebrew and Greek terms that are translated into the English word *love*, but with different meanings.

Aheb is the most common Hebrew word for love in the Old Testament. It is a very broad term and can refer to all sorts of connections and relationships.[1] Look at the examples below and see how different the meaning of *aheb* can be:

- God's care for us. "Because he loved your ancestors, he chose to bless their descendants."[2]

- Our care for one another. "Take your son, your only son—yes, Isaac, whom you love so much . . ."[3]

- Our physical appetites. "If you love sleep, you will end in poverty."[4]

- Romantic and sexual pleasure. "Let her breasts satisfy you always. May you always be captivated by her love."[5]

Phileo, a Greek word used in the New Testament, conveys attraction to someone or something; it is affectionate.[6] For example, "Keep on *loving* each other as brothers and sisters."[7]

Agapao, the dominant Greek New Testament term for love, can refer to care and concern from both the personal and the spiritual sides of life.[8] Jesus' teaching to his disciples is an example: "This is my commandment: *Love* each other in the same way I have *loved* you."[9]

What Do Our Experiences Say about Love?

Our everyday experiences reflect how love is used and understood as well. For example, some people understand love to be essentially an *experience of closeness*. In this view, love is feeling of togetherness and intimacy between two individuals that keeps them coming together with each other. It can be the tenderness of a mother's love for her child. It can be the affection of two long-term close friends. It is a moving and unforgettable emotion. This emotional experience of intimacy is something people search for, focus on, and even sometimes are willing to die for. Everyone needs to know they belong somewhere, in some relationship. In this view, there is a move toward oneness with another person.

Others see love as a way to *encourage and lift others up*. They seek ways to help people know they are valuable and important. They bring comfort to others when they are down. They promote a positive viewpoint and perspective to others. This is the type of person, for example, who is popular among coworkers because he provides energy and optimism to the office environment.

Love is also viewed as *actions that help others*. When we take action and get involved with people, we are proving our love. Our behaviors matter more than our words. In this view, thoughtful and helpful gestures are what convey love: a card, fixing someone's computer, or doing an errand shows love to another. The soldier's sacrifice of life for his country is an example of one of the highest forms of this type of love.

Still others consider *love as equal to romance*. The attraction, sexuality, and attachment of the genders can be intense, gratifying, and extremely pleasurable. We fall in love, are in love or out of love, and make love. In this perspective, love is considered to be synonymous with the experience of romance and sexual passion.

LOVE IS SEEKING AND DOING THE BEST FOR ANOTHER

In this book, I define *love* simply as "seeking and doing the best for another." When we love someone, we bend our heart, mind, and energies toward the betterment of someone else. That is what loving people do. It involves the whole person. It is ongoing and intentional.

This understanding of love is closest in meaning to *aheb* and *agapao*, for it has to do with how we treat each other. That is, at its heart, *love is a value*. A value is something that forms the basis for who you are and how you run your life and relationships. People have values for their finances, such as conservative or aggressive investing values. They have values for their careers, such as concentrating on what they want to accomplish with their gifts and talents. And they have values for their spiritual lives, such as making God a central part of their lives and adhering to the tenets of their theology. Likewise, people have values for their relationships, such as the importance of people in their lives being safe and honest with each other.

> IN THIS BOOK, I DEFINE *LOVE* SIMPLY AS "SEEKING AND DOING THE BEST FOR ANOTHER."

AT ITS HEART, LOVE IS A VALUE.

In other words, love is having a value for doing and being what is most helpful for someone. Its intent is for the betterment, safety, healing, growth, success, and responsible behavior of someone else. It is an others-oriented and others-focused value. It involves actions, words, feelings, and experiences that all come together in love. For example, loving someone could be helping him feel included in a party. It could be providing a listening ear to her hurts. It could be loaning him your car when his is broken down.

LOVE IS SOMETIMES UNCOMFORTABLE

There are also times when what is truly best for someone may not always be what that person *thinks* is best. It could be telling a friend that you don't think the guy she is dating is good for her. Or it could mean taking a job you don't like in order to provide for your family. Loving people become, and do, what is good for people they care about.

As the architect of love, God lives out this definition. He is constantly seeking and doing what is for our best, things that help us connect, grow, and heal. He is actively doing whatever it takes for us to be the people he designed us to be. The ultimate example of his love is, and always will be, in the sacrifice of Jesus for an alienated and broken creation: "For God loved the world so much that he gave his one and only Son, so that everyone who believes in him will not perish but have eternal life."[10] For centuries, the mystery of a love that would move someone to give that much of himself for others has been a profound inspiration and hope for anyone who wants to understand what loving is. But in seeking for, and acting for, our best, God provided his best. And that is often what loving is all about.

So, in this view, love is more than a close feeling and a sense of intimacy with others. In fact, when you love someone the right way, it may have the opposite effect from closeness! Confronting someone who is being hurtful may cause conflict or distance. It may be painful. But let's return to our definition of love: seeking and doing what is best for that person. The easy thing, which is to avoid the confrontation, might seem more loving to your friend, but it would actually be a form of neglect, because your loved one may suffer without your correction.

Realizing that love is for the betterment of others is a good, healthy, and truly caring understanding of love, even though it is not always comfortable. For example, I told my friend Neil that I thought he was being emotionally unfaithful to his wife in his relationship with a coworker. I didn't want to do it. I thought he would really be angry with me. Quite honestly, I dreaded the conversation with him. I did not anticipate any feelings of closeness and intimacy during that conversation, and I was not wrong. Neil was furious with me and thought I was out of line. He withdrew from our relationship for a time. I did not enjoy any of this, but I knew that it was the most loving thing I could do for Neil, his wife, and the other woman.

Long story short, things got better. In time, Neil dealt with the problem. He ended the relationship with his coworker before things went too far. He confessed what was going on to his wife. He got help for the issues that drove that mistake. His marriage became much stronger. And ironically, after we had been through this conflict with each other, Neil and I were connected as friends in a deeper and more intimate way than we had been before. *The feeling of closeness, in this situation, was not the cause but the effect of being a loving person.* Intimacy is sometimes a fruit, more than a root, of love.

> INTIMACY IS SOMETIMES A FRUIT, MORE THAN A ROOT, OF LOVE.

However, this does not mean that love is devoid of warm and tender emotions. There is great depth of feeling involved in love, even when we are in bitter conflict with the person we love. We feel things for them. When they hurt, we hurt. When they are happy, we are happy. When they cause themselves pain, we feel it also. I really felt concern and care for Neil, and that was what prompted me to confront him. And I wanted his best, *even if it jeopardized the closeness I desired with him.* As a loving person, you may have very positive and warm feelings for someone who is angry with you, in the same way a parent sometimes feels toward a child who is enraged at a consequence. So remember, as a loving person you may desire intimacy with someone, but your intimacy with that person may be trumped by your willingness to do the right thing for him.

Coming back to the basic definition of love, when we seek and act on the other's best, the result can be the closeness and intimacy we desire. Yet sometimes it is not. Had Neil been a different man, it may not have. But I hope that I would have still done what was best for him.

LOVE INVOLVES EVERY PART OF US

Feelings are only part of what loving people is all about. The value of seeking and doing the best for the other encompasses every part of us: our thoughts, feelings, behaviors, words, and decisions. Seeking and doing require intentional focus and outcomes. But we must use all parts of ourselves to achieve our goal. Jesus says we are to love God "with all your heart, all your soul, all your mind, and all your strength."[11] We use all those parts to best love God. And as a result, we use all those parts to best love people.

So loving people love emotionally, as well as in values and behavior, in the way God models his love for us. Our values and our emotions are linked in love. They cannot be separated, nor should they. A loving person without feelings cannot fully experience love's power. Conversely, an emotional person without love's direction is a slave to his impulses and desires. A loving person is passionate, is concerned, desires closeness, and is at the same time firmly rooted and grounded in reality and truth.

THE MYTH OF LOVING YOURSELF

You've certainly heard it said that "before you can love someone else, you need to love yourself first." That sounds good, but it is simply not true, and it tends to isolate us from relationship as well. The saying comes from the thinking that you can't provide for others what you can't provide for yourself, and that self-loving people are ultimately more caring. However, the reality is that love is an interpersonal, relational process. It occurs between one person and another, not inside one person. Love requires a subject and an object, and they are different from one another. We can no more love ourselves than we can tell our car to fill itself up with gas from the trunk.

Sometimes people understand Jesus' words to "love your neighbor as yourself" as teaching self-love.[12] Actually, it makes more sense that it teaches that we are to love our neighbor as we would want to be loved—again, a relational meaning.

The answer is, then, to be loved, receive love, experience love. Get it from the outside, and let it change you. That provides what you need to become a loving person.

LOVING PEOPLE ARE GROWING PEOPLE

Being a loving person is not an end in and of itself. People who are learning to care for others are also involved in the growth process, as loving people are growing people. That is, we are to continually be changing, becoming better people, extending ourselves, developing our abilities, healing from any issues we have, and improving ourselves. You can only understand love, and truly become loving in the best way possible, by this process.

Love cannot be fully experienced or developed outside of the context of personal and spiritual growth. Using a computer metaphor, love may be your most important software application. But growth is the operating system that is the framework for all applications to work and function. It is how we should live.

I have several friends who are very caring and loving individuals but seem to have little interest or involvement in personal growth. Though there is no way to prove this, I think their capacity for love is limited by this lack; they would be even deeper and richer in love were they to begin the growth process. That has been my experience with people I have known before and after getting into growth. Growth increases love and our ability to be loving.

Henry Cloud and I conduct an intensive weeklong retreat for leaders several times a year in Southern California, called the Ultimate Leadership Workshop. In this setting, leaders

LOVE CANNOT BE FULLY EXPERIENCED OR DEVELOPED OUTSIDE OF THE CONTEXT OF PERSONAL AND SPIRITUAL GROWTH.

from all aspects of leadership—from the corporate world to small business leaders to pastors, teachers, and ministry leaders—meet to develop their leadership capacities by dealing with their character issues, personality, and inner worlds. The structure of the week incorporates teaching sessions in which Henry and I explain how the leaders' insides affect their outcomes. For example, a leader who is isolated and has problems trusting others may have difficulty in casting vision and connecting with people in his organization. The workshop also incorporates intensive process groups led by professional facilitators. In these groups, which have an emphasis on being a safe setting, leaders can begin to experience what they have been learning from the teaching sessions. The attendees often report breakthrough experiences in which they finally "get it" about some personal issue that has been holding them back. And then, when they return home, they often find that they have new skills, capacities, and ways of relating to others that benefit the organization and also their families. So the workshop is an accelerated setting for continued training and growth of the leader.

I remember one recent workshop week in which I talked to Randall, a pastor who was a very task-oriented, driven, and somewhat obsessive person. He was intelligent and had good and clear motives and values, but he was stuck in the left side of his brain. When he interacted with others, his conversation tended to drift toward goals, logistics, strategies, tasks, and so forth; he had a hard time talking about personal matters and connecting with people at deeper levels. He truly cared about other people, but he didn't know how to show or experience his caring in ways that work best. This is a common issue with leaders, and it was one of the reasons he was in the workshop. Randall was aware that his ability to connect with people had some limitations, and he did not want that to get in the way of his leadership.

When I ran into Randall near the end of the workshop week, I saw a different person. He was much warmer, more responsive, and more connected. I asked him, "How have things gone?" Randall told me what had happened. It turned out that in one of the group sessions, he had become aware that his parents, though they loved him a great deal, were not comfortable with the emotions of their kids, especially the negative ones. So, when he would get upset, they would attempt to reason him out of his feelings by saying things like, "It doesn't do any good to cry; just think good thoughts." Having nowhere to go with his feelings, Randall had grown up a highly skilled and bright thinker who had a hard time connecting and relating.

When he made the connection from his past to his present, the other leaders in his group were warm and compassionate with his experience. They made it safe for him. He told me that when this happened, something broke loose inside him, and some strong emotions began to come out. Randall began to feel emotions he had not known about for years: sadness, joy, anger, grief. They were a little out of his comfort zone, but he stuck with them, the group stuck with him, and he processed the emotions. And he started feeling alive, as though he was a real person.

Once Randall began to deal with this and relate at this level, his relationships with the other leaders in his small group began to change and open up. They were able to get closer to him. As well, he began to listen to them in ways he never had before. He shared experiences, hopes, dreams, and hurts with them. He got beyond vision casting and strategies. And more than one attendee came up to me and told me what a relational person Randall had become.

This is the point: *growth develops the capacity to love.* Randall's experience illustrates how important it is for you to be in the process of growth, dealing with and resolving issues, struggles, problems, and brokenness— little or big, mild or severe. Your capacity to be a loving person will be greatly affected by the extent of your involvement in the life of growth.

THE MORE
CHARACTER
YOU BUILD, THE
GREATER YOUR
ABILITY TO
LOVE AND
PROVIDE FOR
OTHERS.

And that is a huge takeaway for anyone who wants to be loving, because ultimately we are talking about character. Character, defined as that set of abilities we need to meet life's demands, is what makes you loving, unloving, or somewhere in between. People who are involved in personal growth are maturing and strengthening their own character capacities. These will help them succeed in relationships, work, problem solving, and finding their mission in life. *The more character you build, the greater your ability to love and provide for others.* You cannot separate love from who you are inside, so make sure you are working on being a better person inside. Remember that just because you want to care, intend to care, and feel care does not mean you are the loving person you were designed to be. Love is also increased in its capacity, depth, and fruit in others by how we grow and change.

LOVE AND THE BODY

Love is not just in your mind; it is also part of your body. Research seems to indicate that not only is love a spiritual and a developmental matter, but there is also a hardwiring aspect to it. That is, scientists are beginning to tie in attachment and connection to biological and neurological structures and processes. They see a two-way street of interaction between relationships and how the brain develops. Relationships affect the brain, and vice versa. This is exciting research because it suggests that we are designed to connect relationally and personally, from our cells on up, and that relationships are a powerful force in how we grow and develop.

Neurotransmitters in the brain, as well as our hormones, are part of this research. For example, the brain chemicals dopamine, norepinephrine, and serotonin are being associated with drives for connection and romantic attraction. As we interact with each other, we are also going through significant increases and decreases in the amounts of these chemicals.[13]

LOVE IS NOT JUST IN YOUR MIND; IT IS ALSO PART OF YOUR BODY.

Additionally, researchers have identified brain substances called mirror neurons, and there is a great deal of scientific interest in them. In animal studies, these neurons fire the same way when the subject either performs an act or observes someone else doing the same thing. For example, the same result occurs when the animals both eat food and watch another one eat. As research is beginning with humans now, one possibility is that neurons might be involved in the way we empathize. In other words, seeing someone's emotions might generate a similar emotional response in us, supported by the activity of the mirror neurons. There is much unknown at this point, but it is exciting to see how we might be designed for connection.[14]

Not only that, but genetic researchers are addressing relationships as well.

They are making connections between how individuals make or don't make attachments, looking at the possibilities of certain gene factors that influence this. For example, there may be a genetic tendency toward loneliness.[15]

In addition, there is a great deal of research supporting the idea that love, in and of itself, promotes well-being and health in general. Secure relationships, for example, have been shown to help people deal with adversity, recover more quickly from stressful life events, and experience increased immune functioning.[16] And on the negative side, loneliness can speed up our natural physical decline as we age.[17] Loving people are not only doing the right thing; they are living the right life.

We need to be encouraged about this information, especially because of how it supports the idea in the Bible that a life lived the way God designed for us, connected to each other and connected to him as he tells us to, results in good things for us: "If you obey all the decrees and commands I am giving you today, all will be well with you and your children. I am giving you these instructions *so you will enjoy a long life* in the land the LORD your God is giving you for all time."[18] However, none of these findings should lead us to conclude that love is determined by chemistry or heritage, and that we have no say in our tendencies toward or against relationships. We still have responsibility and choices, no matter what the impact of our biology. The burden of love does not change, nor does our ownership of it.

LOVING THE UNLOVABLE

One of the most important realities of the nature of love is that the "lovability" of the other person is ultimately irrelevant. Said another way, *the more we require that the other person be lovable in order for us to care, the less loving we are.* The converse is also true: the less we require the person to be lovable, the more loving we are.

This is not an easy reality, but it is true just the same. It is certainly much more natural to care about those who care for us. But what is natural is not always what is mature and what is best. For example, my friend Donna is married to a man named Dylan, who can be quite self-centered and controlling. Dylan has been unkind to Donna, though he rarely admits or owns it when he does. He is not abusive or unfaithful, but he has some major character issues and has been very difficult to live with. Many of Donna's friends have advised her to leave him, because they care about her and don't like how he treats her. "He obviously doesn't care about you," they say. "And there is no indication that he will change."

Donna and I have talked often about her relationship with Dylan. He is not a very lovable person. I like him in a casual way, the way that you can like someone from a distance, but I have a hard time getting close to him. He is not easy to connect with, and, beyond being a stable provider and having similar spiritual values and interests, he doesn't offer Donna much at all. She has considered leaving the relationship, as it has been very painful for her. Yet she has stayed in the marriage and has committed to being his wife. When she is asked why, she says, "Well, for more than one reason. I believe that marriage is for better or worse. I have spiritual values about marriage that are important guides to me. And I love Dylan."

THE MORE WE REQUIRE THAT THE OTHER PERSON BE LOVABLE IN ORDER FOR US TO CARE, THE LESS LOVING WE ARE.

Donna is telling the truth—she really loves him. I have witnessed this. She cares about him and his life. She listens to him. She supports his activities and interests. She is involved in making a good life with him and their friends. She is kind to him. When together with them, I have seen him talk about some difficulty in his life and watched tears come to her eyes for what he goes through. She is a remarkable person. I think that Dylan probably does have some love for Donna, in the sense of seeking and doing what is best for the other person. But I also think that she loves Dylan, using this definition of the word, more than he loves her. That happens in any relationship. This is not a put-down of Dylan; it is just an observation of the relationship.

Donna would not say that she is "in love" with Dylan at this point, though that might change if he ever changes. But she is concerned about and cares for this man. Now, she is not in denial about him. Nor is she an unrealistically hopeful optimist. In addition, she does not put up with his hurtfulness and has strict boundaries with that. She will not allow unkind treatment that wounds her. If Dylan ever does become a more lovable person, it will be due in large part to a wife who stood by her husband and loved him from her heart, in reality, and thoroughly.

Donna's example illustrates the point about lovability. In other words, people who truly love someone do so because of what is inside them, not because of good qualities inside the other person. I cannot overstate the significance of this for you as you learn these principles. When you can empathize and have compassion for someone who is selfish, unkind, or hurtful, you are becoming a truly loving and growing person.

There is nothing wrong with moving toward someone who cares and loves you back. Lovable people are grateful. They love in return. They want to give to us. They make the work of loving pleasurable and deeply meaningful. A mutually caring and loving relationship is one of the richest experiences in the world. By the same token, it is also normal to avoid or withdraw from a controlling or defensive person. They make the relationship more work. They may not appreciate what you are doing. They may reject your approaches and even reject you as a person. But *what is normal is not always what is truly loving.* What is normal may be the equivalent of the thinking of a three-year-old: *I'll be nice to you if you are nice to me. But if you aren't nice, I won't be nice to you.* The world does not turn out as well if we all have that mentality. It's just not how grown-ups are to live.

Ultimately, this is an important issue not only in relationships but also in theology. The three-year-old mentality mentioned above is what theologians would describe as someone living under the law—that is, eye for eye and tooth for tooth. A person living under the law says, "I will treat you as you treat me. If you are lovable, I will love you. If not, I will withdraw love." But living under grace, and understanding love's nature, fulfills all the law's requirements. It provides a higher and better path. Consider these words of Jesus:

You have heard the law that says, "Love your neighbor" and hate your enemy. But I say, love your enemies! Pray for those who persecute you! In that way, you will be acting as true children of your Father in heaven. For he gives his sunlight to both the evil and the good, and he sends rain on the just and the unjust alike. If you love only those who love you, what reward is there for that? Even corrupt tax collectors do that much. If you are kind only to your friends, how are you different from anyone else? Even pagans do that. But you are to be perfect, even as your Father in heaven is perfect.[19]

Jesus said a lot of difficult things, and this is certainly one of them. But the point is that love should be based on your concern for the needs and betterment of the other and not how much they appreciate us, for that is how God is with us. In reality, love is at its best, and you are at your best, when you care about people who are not very lovable. This is because those are the ones who need it most.

You may think, *He doesn't deserve my love, with what he has done.* And you may be right. That is the point. No one deserves love. Not you. Not me. Not the "good guy". *No one deserves love, but everyone needs love.* And the

> IN REALITY, LOVE IS AT ITS BEST, AND YOU ARE AT YOUR BEST, WHEN YOU CARE ABOUT PEOPLE WHO ARE NOT VERY LOVABLE.

unkind, self-centered, destructive people in your life are so bereft of love that they often need a miracle to get them out of their mess. And that is what the good news of Christ is all about: "For Christ died for sins once for all, the righteous for the unrighteous, to bring you to God."[20] It is our very state of unrighteousness that moved God's heart to reach out and love us in an unfathomable way.

This is important to understand in relationships. When you truly love someone in a mature way, you seek the person's best, but you also seek the person, as much as that is possible. That is, love goes further than tolerating someone or having the ability to stand being in his or her presence. That certainly may be all you can do in a very difficult relationship, and that is good. But as you grow in your ability to become a loving person, you will find that you can, over time, "love the sinner and hate the sin," as the old preachers say. And the reason this is important is that *unlovable people, like all people, need to be sought, not tolerated.* Everybody needs to be sought after in love. God sought us out while we were shaking our fists at him, because he knew we needed this. That is how we are to be toward others.

DO NOT CONFUSE LOVING WITH ENABLING

Please don't misunderstand this point. You may be in a relationship with a person who has been really hurtful with you. It may take your maximum and best effort, right now, to be as kind and considerate as you can, though that may not seem like a lot to you. It may indeed be a great deal, and you are to be commended for that. You may have to set limits and consequences with someone to guard yourself from their issues. That is a good thing. We are not to allow or promote irresponsibility or hurtful behavior with others at all, as much as possible.

> NO ONE DESERVES LOVE, BUT EVERYONE NEEDS LOVE.

When I write books on setting boundaries in relationships, work, or life in general, I am always thinking of how to help people see the benefits of taking ownership over their lives and have more freedom, self-control, and better relationships. And part of that thinking has to do with nipping things in the bud that are harmful, such as controlling behaviors, bad treatment, addictions, abuse, and the like. *And it includes increasing your capacity to freely love and care about someone else.* You need boundaries in order to help you protect and guard yourself from harm and to help others learn to take responsibility for their emotions and behaviors. And that increases your ability to choose, take ownership, and care.

So make sure of this: *do not confuse the grace of being loving with the license of being enabling.* Loving people don't put up with evil and foolishness. That is enabling and rescuing, and it never helps anyone. Instead, people who are truly loving will confront, limit, and quarantine people who consistently make wrong choices. So keep that distinction in mind: love seeks the best, but it does not enable bad behavior.

But with all this said, remember that as you grow into a more loving person, you will seek good for that person and wish good things for that person. It may have to be from a distance, with some separateness, especially if the person is very toxic, and you must be responsible for yourself. But loving people still go further than merely tolerating an unlovable person as the person continues to grow in love and grace.

Not only that, but loving a lovable person requires no real growth, grace, effort, or transformation on our part. As I said, loving those who are lovable is easy. We are drawn to them, and we also draw from them. But think now about a toxic person in your life, even one who has caused you pain or injury. And think about the prospect of seeking and doing what is best for that person. That is a different matter. Most of us would instead recall bad memories and desires for justice and revenge. This is not to say that there should not be justice; justice is important and may even be a form of love the person truly needs to experience. But the point is, when you grow in your capacity to love, you will find yourself caring about people in your life with less regard to how lovable they are.

LOVE SEEKS THE BEST, BUT IT DOESN'T ENABLE BAD BEHAVIOR.

And the ultimate fruit of learning to love that selfish or hurtful person can often be a miracle: *your love can help them, the unlovable, to become more lovable*. The safety, acceptance, and care you bring to unlovable people may be part of a recipe that God has for them, which can produce inside them what does not exist. That is one of the great things love does—it promotes good for both the giver and the receiver.

LOVING PEOPLE ARE HATING PEOPLE TOO

As you grow in becoming a loving person, you will find that your capacity to care, have empathy, and connect with others will also develop and increase. However, sometimes people are often concerned that they also get angry or even hateful. They may feel primarily warm and positive toward a spouse, friend, or family member. Then, when a problem occurs, they may also experience frustrated and resentful emotions. It is then common for a person to wonder if he or she is truly a loving person: *If I were loving, wouldn't I be less negative?*

So you may be questioning your own loving nature: *Do anger and hatred destroy love that is inside me?* To understand this, we need to clarify the terms. Anger and hatred are not the same thing.

ANGER

Anger is an emotion. Like all emotions, it serves as a signal to us, giving us information we need. Feelings are like the warning alerts on your computer screen. They pop up when your battery is down, when a virus is present, or when your hard drive is full. That way, you know it is time to do something. In the same way, the emotion of anger pops up to signal us that there is a problem to be solved. There is action to be taken about some matter. The angry feelings generate energy, awareness, and focus so that we can move quickly to fix whatever is going on.

Just as computer alerts are neither good nor bad in themselves, anger is also morally neutral. What drives us to anger can be good or bad. For example, my sons now have the same shoe size as I do, so sometimes they will ask to borrow my dress shoes for some formal function, such as a banquet. The other day, I could not find my black dress shoes, and I searched for them frantically because I had to speak at an event. I got mad at my kids, thinking they had borrowed my shoes without checking with me. I figured that after I got home I would sit them down and let them know how difficult they had made things for me. I had worked all this out in my mind. Then I found the shoes in my luggage because I had forgotten to unpack them from a trip. Now, instead of being bugged with my sons, I was bugged at myself for judging them. The direction changed. What is underneath and drives our anger is the important thing.

Sometimes we become angry because something good and valuable is in danger—such as a person we love, our hard-earned money, or our own feelings—and we want to take action to protect it. That is a good and helpful use of anger. If you are trying to be close to someone who continually attacks your opinion and feelings, it makes sense to get mad at the attack. You are having protective feelings toward the relationship and your emotions, and that is what the anger is telling you to do. This anger helps you to solve problems and take actions in your relationships.

But we also become angry because something we have no right to have in the first place is being taken from us. For example, our spouse has had a bad day and can't listen to our day very attentively. Or our kids do not want to go to the movies when we want to, preferring to be with their friends that night.

When we get angry because someone else has choices, our anger is self-centered and unhelpful. We need to let go of this anger and move on from it.

Old hurts. In addition, anger toward someone can be simply a sign that the person is important to you. That is, someone you care about can bother you more than a stranger can, because the person is close to your heart. For example, I have a friend, Roger, who is one of the most patient, easygoing people I know. I have seen him in business meetings when tempers have flared, and he is the voice of reason and sanity. He does not take things personally, and things roll off his back—except with his older brother, Burt. Burt can get to Roger without much effort at all. Burt will talk with a certain disrespectful tone to Roger or make fun of him in subtle ways. And Roger will go off as though he has been electrocuted. He gets angry, faces off with Burt, and feels quite disrespected by him. I asked Roger about this, after seeing it happen. He described a long-term love/hate relationship with his brother. For much of their history, Roger felt put down and dismissed by Burt. And Burt still seems to regard Roger in negative ways. Roger, who is unruffled by almost anyone, has unfinished business that comes out with his brother. And this illustrates the reality that we often get angrier with those important to us than those to whom we are not so close.

A sign of your own struggle. Sometimes we even get mad at people we care about simply because we are not doing that well, not because they have done anything wrong or mean to us. In other words, sometimes our anger may be more about us than it is about them. Our loved ones are just a safer and bigger target for our anger. I remember leading a group in which one man, Bill, seemed to have it out for another member, Dave. Bill and Dave were very different people. While Bill had major struggles in his marriage and career, Dave's were less severe. He had issues he was working on, but he had a good marriage and liked his career. This was not pretense on Dave's part; he was just a nice person who was in a good stage of life.

Interaction and honest confrontation are important parts of helpful groups, so the members did a lot of that with each other. Bill and Dave liked each other and, like everyone else in the group, practiced telling the truth in love to each other. It seemed to be a valuable relationship for both of them. But during a period of several sessions, however, I noticed a change in the normal pattern between the two. Bill apparently just had it in for Dave. He was like a pit bull with him. Bill confronted Dave about a number of slights that didn't seem real. For example, he said, "When I was talking last week, you turned the topic back to yourself." Another time he said, "You think you have it all together, and I can tell you feel superior." And then there was, "You gave me a critical look when I spoke."

Dave was at first taken aback and did his best to see if he was actually doing all these things. He tried to be open to Bill's observations. He asked for more specific feedback from Dave and for the group's impressions of each situation, things all people should do when confronted about matters. But each time he came up empty, as did the group and myself. We couldn't see that Bill's confrontations were founded in reality. Finally, after another angry confrontation from Bill, I asked, "Bill, is it possible that what you are really saying to Dave is, 'I want to matter to you'?"

SOMETIMES OUR ANGER MAY BE MORE ABOUT US THAN IT IS ABOUT THEM.

"What do you mean?" Bill asked.

"Well, I don't see a lot of reality in what you are saying to Dave. And I know you are going through some very difficult circumstances right now. And maybe you don't know if a guy like Dave, who is doing OK right now, can care about you in your present state. I was wondering if you aren't sure about how strong your relationship is with Dave."

Bill sat there for a few seconds silently. The group could tell something important was happening inside him, so they waited, supporting him quietly. Finally, Bill said, "OK. I think I get this. This makes sense."

He turned to Dave. "I do like you, and our friendship. You matter to me. You are a good guy, and I admire you. But my life is not working well right now. And I think it's hard to imagine that you could really give a rip about me, as screwed up as my life is now."

Bill understood. In fact, as we progressed further, it became clear that he was condemning himself and projecting those feelings on Dave, expecting Dave to feel toward him the way he felt toward himself.

Here was Dave's response: "Thanks for saying that; I feel better about us now. I had no idea what was going on between us. And I am really sorry about how bad you have been feeling lately. I want to know more about it, buddy, and I want to help you through this. I don't know what I'd do without you in this group." With that, the conflict began to resolve, and we went on to other people and other issues. The point is, Bill was in a lot of pain, and he directed his anger toward Dave. Had Dave not been so important to Bill, I do not think this interaction would have happened.

HATRED

Hatred is different from anger. While anger is an emotion, and emotions are transitory and can change quickly, hatred is a stance. It has no real time limit to it. Hatred indicates that you wish someone ill or desire revenge or pain for them. It is more of a value and attitude than an emotion. Hatred can destroy love and relationship. That is, if you dislike someone so intensely that you find yourself wishing the person harm, or that he will fail in life, it is anti-love, the opposite of seeking and accomplishing the person's best.

Often, hatred that will not go away has other causes that keep it alive. For example, a lack of forgiveness, a relationship in which we feel helpless and controlled, our resistance to the freedoms of others, and our envy of the success of others are common roots of hatred. We need to be aware of, and take responsibility for, our wishes to take revenge on and hurt those with whom we are in conflict. We need to identify these feelings and then let them go.

There is a necessary hatred in love, however. This sort of hatred can, in fact, be a very good thing, as it is meant to help us guard things that would destroy love forever. While wishing a loved one harm will do you no good, at the same time, *there are things that you, as a loving person, should really hate!* We do well to hate things that stand in the way of love. In fact, if we do not hate

WHILE ANGER IS AN EMOTION . . . HATRED IS A STANCE.

the right things, it can compromise our ability to truly love. That is the way God is inside his heart. He cannot stand things that hurt the good he wants to see in the world. In that way, hatred and anger are similar. If they are for protecting love and goodness, they are helpful. If they are for selfishness or hurting others, they are destructive.

Take a look at this list below. Just as God has things he loves, he also has a "hate list." Here are just a few of the things the Bible tells us God hates:

- "There are six things the LORD hates—no, seven things he detests: haughty eyes, a lying tongue, hands that kill the innocent, a heart that plots evil, feet that race to do wrong, a false witness who pours out lies, a person who sows discord in a family."[21]

- "For I, the LORD, love justice. I hate robbery and wrongdoing."[22]

- "Don't scheme against each other. Stop your love of telling lies that you swear are the truth. I hate all these things, says the LORD."[23]

- "'For I hate divorce!' says the Lord, the God of Israel. 'To divorce your wife is to overwhelm her with cruelty,' says the LORD of Heaven's Armies. 'So guard your heart; do not be unfaithful to your wife.'"[24]

- "Don't just pretend to love others. Really love them. Hate what is wrong. Hold tightly to what is good."[25]

The above list reveals that God hates anything that hurts love, goodness, and innocence. His hatred protects and guards love from harm. So learn to become a loving person who hates what God hates. It will help clarify and define you in order for you to love what he loves also. As I said earlier, "Love the sinner and hate the sin." And realize that we need the same grace that we are to give to others.

THERE ARE THINGS THAT YOU, AS A LOVING PERSON, SHOULD REALLY HATE!

THE REALITY: WE FAIL SOMETIMES

We are never truly finished with changing emotionally and spiritually, though we can make great changes and strides toward becoming a healthy, loving person. That means that, along with the proper and righteous anger and hatred we need, loving people will still slip up and be selfishly mad and revengeful toward others they love. While that is not a good thing, it is a real thing.

So do not expect yourself to never be angry with those you love; do not be totally disappointed with yourself when you fail. Keep working on demonstarting love and healthy expressions of anger and hatred, while giving up the unhealthy versions. However, in your mind, and in your loving relationships, there needs to be more love than anger and hate. This mix has to always be increasing on the love side of the formula as you grow and mature. Otherwise there is not enough connection and care to digest, deal with, resolve, and metabolize the negatives.

No matter what emotion you may currently feel toward your loved ones, love must be the most dominant. I encourage people to tell those in their lives, "I love you and I get mad at you, but the love is greater than the mad." That is what real and growing relationships are about.

THE MYTH OF BEING DRAINED

It is important at the outset of a book on love to clarify the widespread myth that when you love people, you will be emptied, drained, and sucked dry. Many people are concerned about this, afraid that if they give of themselves too much, they may get in trouble emotionally or not have enough care to give to others they are responsible for, or even enough to take care of themselves. For example, a friend of mine who is a nurse in the intensive care unit at a hospital told me she was thinking about changing her career, as it took too much away from her. "After an eight-hour shift, there's nothing left of me, and then I have to care for my family. But I don't have anything left to give," she said. There are other serving, relationally based careers that have this issue, such as teaching, ministry, counseling, and the like. This is a common concern. However, it is based on some faulty ideas. Since I do not want you to avoid taking the risk and effort of becoming a loving person, I want to clarify the realities in this area.

Love Is Not a Substance but an Internal Ability

In my writing and speaking, I often use the metaphor of "love is fuel" to clarify how we need to both receive it and give it. However, that metaphor is not 100 percent accurate. We do not receive a gallon of care and give a gallon of care. It is not a one-to-one ratio.

There will be times you deeply care about another person and come away energized, hopeful, and happy that you have had the experience. I have often had this happen and felt just as "full" as the person with whom I was connecting. If love were a substance, I would feel emptier as they felt filled up, but that is often not the case at all. Love can truly be win-win. How many times have you heard about someone helping a person in trouble who later says about the experience, "I gave to this person, but I ended up receiving love in return as well"?

THE MORE LOVING YOU BECOME, THE MORE LOVING YOU CAN BE

Loving people become competent and skillful at love. They know how to care, how to help, and how to heal. And they do this better and better as time goes on. Rather than going through life and having to scale down on connecting, loving people increase their abilities and capacities.

I know individuals in their seventies and beyond who are not constrained and limited by their hearts, only by their bodies. The physical machine may be slowing down and wearing down, but their attentiveness, understanding, and care are greater than they ever were. Don't be afraid of losing love as you give it . . . love increases as you give it.

MOST "DRAIN" PROBLEMS COME FROM OTHER SOURCES

Certainly, people do burn out and feel drained by their connections with others. But do not lay the blame for that at the feet of love. There are other reasons for the feeling of being drained by another person.

Codependency. The "need to be needed" problem, codependency is the tendency to take responsibility for others' lives, unhappiness, problems, or character immaturity. Whether it is motivated by concern, guilt, or a lack of understanding, codependency results in rescuing or enabling behaviors. If you tend to be codependent in your relationships, I guarantee you will feel drained at some point.

There is a reason that those who enable others feel drained. Codependents take ownership of problems that another person should be worried about. They are actually shouldering a burden that is not theirs to bear. It does not fit, it is not right, and it harms them and the person they want to help by regressing that person and removing them from accountability for their life. Codependents are taking on the wrong tasks, while the other person is not taking them at all. That is why, if you find yourself more concerned about another person's problems than the person is, it is likely that you are codependent.

For example, suppose your spouse has an anger problem. He gets mad at little things, he explodes, and he uses anger to control relationships. He has two internal gears: OK and mad. If you came to me and asked for help with the issue, I would ask, "Who is more concerned about this issue: your spouse or you? Is he saying, 'Look, I blow up and I hate myself for doing it, but I can't stop. I can't stand what it is doing to you and the kids. I'm going to get some answers and some help. Please be patient with me'?

"Or is he saying, 'It's not that bad. You're overreacting. Anyway, you provoke it, and I wouldn't do it if you weren't so naggy'—while you read books about it, talk to friends, look online for answers, and do all the rest of the search?"

LOVING PEOPLE BECOME COMPETENT AND SKILLFUL AT LOVE.

If you said it is the latter, then we would work on you changing things so that your spouse can become more concerned. The problem will not go away until the person doing it is worried about it. Can you see how drained codependency can make us? That is a large part of the thinking that my book *Who's Pushing Your Buttons?* addresses in detail—how to deal with someone's issues in a realistic and less codependent way.[26]

Loving is not codependency. You cannot love others too much; it is just not possible. But you can take too much ownership over another's life. That is very possible and very destructive for you. So, while we are to love people unreservedly, we are to be careful and clear about taking responsibility and ownership for their actions.

An unconnected state. This phrase *unconnected* refers to the reality that some people do not possess enough love inside to sustain them. They want to care, and do, but there is a lack of comfort, empathy, and grace inside themselves. They are unloved. An unloved state is a way of existing. It is different from having a bad day or a fight with your best friend. Those are transitory. An unloved state doesn't go away until it is dealt with.

People who have this issue often feel drained by the needs and concerns of others. They simply are trying to survive themselves, and they don't have enough to continue on very well. When they are able to do the work to enter the loved state, they hit a threshold. They are able, once they have enough of an internal sense of being loved, to give and give and give (again, not rescuing!), and their internal state of being loved continues. It is difficult for loved people to be drained by caring, while it is easy for unloved people to truly give out of energy, motivation, and love itself.

"Tired" is not "drained." I am not saying that loving people is not work. It is. Loving requires effort, concentration, skill, and the ability to do your part to make an intimate and real connection with another person. There are few things not worth the work involved. But any work makes us tired. So it is no surprise when, at the end of a busy day being involved in connecting, listening, guiding, and the like, loving people need rest. Any effort, even if we receive much from it, will require that. That is what rest is all about. But that is very different from the experience of being empty, drained, and sucked dry. Loving people get tired, and then they must rest.

> YOU CANNOT LOVE OTHERS TOO MUCH; IT IS JUST NOT POSSIBLE. BUT YOU CAN TAKE TOO MUCH OWNERSHIP OVER ANOTHER'S LIFE.

And after resting, they look forward to the relationships in which they are involved. But if you dread reconnecting with people, that may indicate a problem that goes beyond fatigue.

DOING AND HELPING IN LOVE

Let's return for a moment to the active doing and helping aspects of love. It is important not to misunderstand how significant this is. I am referring to the individual who shows his love by being there for other people in tangible, measurable, and sometimes physical ways. This could be the neighbor who is handy and shows up with his tools to help you with your fence. It could be the businessperson who finds a mortgage broker who gives you a very good deal. Or the person who volunteers to baby-sit your kids for an afternoon so you can get away.

In our neighborhood, a teenager named Jack was diagnosed with cancer.

His parents have three other kids and busy lives, but they immediately stopped everything to get Jack the medical help, support, and treatment he needed. Word got around quickly, and with e-mail lists and phone calls, the community surrounded Jack and his family in helpful ways. They brought meals, took kids to the hospital to visit Jack, did errands, and tried to take the pressure off the family so they could focus on Jack's welfare. Over and over again, the parents expressed how overwhelmed and grateful they were for the thoughtful, hands-on love they experienced from their neighbors.

The reason it is easy to miss the importance of doing and helping is the stereotype of the guy who is not good with words or relationships but who shows his feelings and care through helping out. This expression of love is sometimes not as appreciated by those who are more comfortable in the world of words, emotions, and relational connections. I think there is a little one-upmanship going on with those who can verbalize compassion and empathy. This is a mistake. While there is no question that the person who is unfamiliar with feelings and intimacy needs to experience and learn these skills, at the same time, love is as love does, and our actions have import and meaning.

LOVE IS AS LOVE DOES, AND OUR ACTIONS HAVE IMPORT AND MEANING.

I have seen people who really were "there" emotionally with others, and connected deeply, then the next day would forget to call, or miss a meeting, or just not show up in the relationship again. Though the intent was good, the follow-through was not. The point is, you need both to be a fully loving person. Learn how to develop relationships, and also learn practical faithfulness as well.

TAKING THE NEXT STEPS

Keep in mind these principles on the nature of love. It will be helpful to particularly keep in mind the definition: *love* is "seeking and doing the best for another." That will help anchor your thoughts to the other aspects of love in this book. At this point, you will learn the first thing anyone who wants to be a loving person must engage in: becoming a *loved person*.

Let's review a few of the big ideas here, because if you are clear about this part, it will help you make better use of the other sections. Remember the definition of love: seeking and doing what is best for the other. You were hardwired by God to love, so it is part of your nature. Love is inextricably connected to the personal growth process. Finally, remember that loving people also feel anger and hatred. It is just as important to experience the right kinds of anger and hatred that serve love's purposes.

To continue your own path to being a loving person, here are a few tips that will help:

- Ask God for help. The designer of love will not withhold this ability from you. Pray for growth in love.

- Commit yourself to growing in love. Remember the simple definition and keep it in mind daily.

- Find a growth context for yourself. Loving people are not isolated people. They open up to other people who care and will commit to them.

- Look for others who need to be loved. Begin to look at both the lovable and unlovable people in your life as those who need what you can offer.

Finally, a word of encouragement: you will not find many other endeavors that provide a better benefit for your efforts than cultivating the art of loving people. Any time and energy you spend in learning to be a loving person will always bring forth good results for yourself and for those around you.

PART 2

The Key Aspects of Love

THREE

Connecting: Bridging the Gap

I will never forget the evening I experienced the true power of connecting. I was at a dinner party with my wife. As it happened, we were seated with Nicole and Amanda, two of our good friends. Nicole lives near us, and Amanda lives in another part of the country but was in town to visit with the hosts of the party. Nicole and Amanda did not know each other, so I introduced them. Nicole happens to be someone who is able to reach out and get to know others at a very authentic and deep level, in a very brief time. This is just what she does—she connects.

I watched as Nicole, in a very natural manner, showed interest in Amanda and began asking her questions. I think the conversation started with what Amanda did for a living or how she knew the hosts of the party, something that most conversations tend to begin with. But I could see that Nicole really was interested in Amanda and wanted to know her.

Amanda responded. She opened up and began to tell Nicole personal things about her life that even I didn't know about. She told Nicole about her desire to have another child and what a loss it was to find that it wasn't possible. About her plans to become a professional musician someday. About her relationship with her own mother, which was a very painful one. They both became emotional and tearful at times as Nicole responded to Amanda's story.

I was amazed at how quickly Amanda let Nicole in to her deeper self. They were conversing at a level you generally expect with people who have known each other for a while, with a certain amount of time and safety. But Nicole's interest and warmth continued to work on Amanda.

I knew it would be intrusive to keep listening, as the conversation was getting more and more private, and they were getting closer to one another. So I talked to other people at the table and checked in on Nicole and Amanda from time to time.

ONE OF THE BEST THINGS THAT LOVING PEOPLE DO IS TO CONNECT WITH OTHERS.

The party ended, everyone said their good-byes, and Nicole and Amanda hugged and exchanged contact information. A few weeks later I was talking to Amanda on the phone. During our talk, she said, "Thanks for introducing me to Nicole."

"Looks like you two hit it off."

"Yes, she is a pretty amazing person. We've talked a couple of times since I flew back home. I hope we can keep up the friendship in some way. She is special."

"I think so too."

"It isn't easy for me to open up to people; I've always been a little reserved. But that night at the party it seemed like I wanted to let her know about the important things I feel. That kind of talk doesn't come around a lot."

I said, "Neither does that kind of person."

"I know. And even though I haven't known Nicole very long, I feel like I'm a better person for being around her."

There is a postscript here: the two have been friends for years now. With the distance, they don't see each other often. But when they do connect, it is meaningful. And whenever I talk to Amanda, she always says, "Say hi to Nicole when you see her."

HEART TO HEART

Nicole has made a permanent and positive impact on Amanda. She considers herself a better person for the few hours she spent with her. That is the value and the importance of connection.

In this chapter I will show you that one of the best things that loving people do is to connect with others. When you learn the principles and skills of connecting, you can make a difference in the lives of others. You can make great relationships and attachments. And you can draw people to yourself. As an example, I know many people who have had similar experiences with Nicole. She is one of those individuals whom people seek out, for no other reason than to be around her warmth.

What is connection? The best working definition of *connection* is *a heart-to-heart attachment that goes beyond knowing about someone to actually knowing that person.* We are not really connected until the heart comes into play. We live in the gap of isolation and aloneness. Connection bridges that gap.

The most important things in your life reside in your heart. In fact, we are truly alive to the extent that our heart is connected to relationship. If it is disconnected and alone, we may be surviving but not really living. That is how loving and living are connected. One does not exist without the other.

The apostle Paul's words to his close friends in Corinth show the heart and emotion he felt for them and desired from them: "Oh, dear Corinthian friends! We have spoken honestly with you, and our hearts are open to you. There is no lack of love on our part, but you have withheld your love from us. I am asking you to respond as if you were my own children. Open your hearts to us!"[1] He is saying that knowing each other is not sufficient; there must be a heart connection for the relationship to be complete. What was true centuries ago is also true today for you and for those in your life.

> CONNECTION OFTEN BEGINS THE PROCESS OF LOVE IN TIME AND SEQUENCE.

Connection is often the first part of love—that is, connection often begins the process of love in time and sequence. People bond, and if things go well, they then move into a deeper and more truly loving relationship, one in which they are seeking and doing what is best for each other. We are by nature connection seekers. We want to belong, to be attached. But connecting is not the final goal; it is only a part of love.

We will spend more time on the connecting aspect of love than any other in this book. This is because of the need I see in people when I counsel, teach, and speak. So many individuals who want to love do not have the experiences, understanding, or tools they need to make the connections that work in relationships. So this chapter will break that down for you.

There is another reason this is such a developed chapter, and that has to do with the nature of connection itself. It is a bridge. As a bridge, connecting with others can carry and convey other things from one person to another. In that way, connection helps you learn and grow in the other areas of love in this book: truth-telling, healing, letting go, and romance. As you become a connector, you are more able to become the other things you need to be a loving person.

BREAKING DOWN THE ELEMENTS

There are several key elements of our character and makeup that are involved in connection. When we connect, we bring these aspects of ourselves into relationship with others:

- *Feelings.* When we are connected, we can share the emotions we experience about things and people, present and past, whether pleasant or painful.

- *Dreams and desires.* Another part of connection involves sharing our deepest longings and wishes—the things we keep protected and share with only a few friends.

- *Fears.* We are all afraid of something, and connection makes it safe enough to share our fears openly.

- *Failures.* No one is without mistakes, and when we connect, we let others in on the darker parts of our lives.

- *Past.* We all have losses and joys in our pasts, and connection means that we want to bring someone else into our personal history.

- *The other person.* One of the deepest aspects of connection is to let the other person know how you feel and make it safe enough that the relationship is not threatened by this, but rather, strengthened.

- *God and spirituality.* What we know and experience about God is one of the most intimate things we can convey to another person. When we share our spiritual side, we are letting someone in.

Many people are alienated and disconnected from some part of themselves, and that part, in return, is then disconnected from people. Loving people help others by connecting with them. They are able to create a bridge over the chasm of alienation and distance we all feel in this world. And they are able to then cross the bridge they have created so that there is contact between two individuals. When you reach out and connect, you have brought someone out of isolation, loneliness, fear, or detachment into the world of relationship. In this chapter you will learn the principles and skills of this important aspect of being a loving person.

Most of the time, you know when you have connected with another person. This kind of experience is described in various ways. Some people will say, "He gets it about me" or "She understands me" or "I can talk to him about anything and it's OK." Or even, "I don't have to explain myself with her." All these reflect that a heart-to-heart attachment has been made.

CONNECTING PEOPLE ARE
CONNECTED PEOPLE

The best connectors are those who have also been on the receiving end of connection: connecting people are connected people. The Nicoles of the world are not just gifted; they receive the bonding that they can then provide. This only makes sense in that we can provide best what we have experienced and been a part of.

Kyle, a successful businessman, is an example of this. "I think I'm the problem," Kyle told me. "Nancy is the one who wanted this meeting, and she's probably right. Whatever I'm supposed to be doing for her in the marriage, it's not working." Nancy nodded.

Kyle and Nancy had asked to talk to me about their marriage. She was concerned because she didn't feel that the two of them were connected emotionally.

She saw the marriage as supportive and positive, but somewhat distant and not connected. She loved Kyle and saw him as a man with good values who wanted the best for her and the family. But she did not feel they were really attached to each other.

This was confusing and difficult for Kyle. As far as he was concerned, he and Nancy had a very good marriage, and he couldn't understand what she thought she was missing. "I love Nancy," he said. "I tell her all the time. I ask her about her day when I get home from work. I send her flowers. We go out on date nights. I try to pick activities she'll like. I'm not perfect, but I just don't get what is going wrong."

> **CONNECTING PEOPLE ARE CONNECTED PEOPLE.**

On her part, Nancy was feeling discouraged and somewhat helpless. She said, "I don't want to be critical of Kyle; he's the nicest guy in the world. He is kind to me and the kids. But when I try to get close to him, he just shuts down."

I turned to Kyle. "Nancy's talking about emotional intimacy," I said. "What is your understanding of that?"

"Kindness, support, those sorts of things," Kyle replied.

"There is nothing wrong with those things," I said. "I believe that you want to give them to Nancy, and even think you are doing that, but it's not really happening. I think your ability to truly love Nancy, in the way she needs to be loved, is limited."

Kyle did not look as though we were on the same page. So I asked, "When you were young, how did your family connect?"

"I come from a very good family. We learned to treat people right, to be kind, and to help others. We were very loving."

Nancy interjected. "Your parents are very nice people. I do like them. But it has always seemed to me that they have been more interested in what you do than how you feel inside."

Before he could respond, I asked Kyle, "OK, give me an example of a problem or loss you experienced when you were growing up, something that was important to you."

He thought for a minute. "Well, I was a really good shortstop in high school. I thought I had a shot at playing college ball, and maybe going beyond that, who knew. Scouts were showing up at my games, and everybody in the school was pretty excited. We all knew something big was going to happen in my baseball life. Then in my senior year I injured my shoulder pretty badly, and it was all over."

"That would be a big deal. How did that feel?"

"It was terrible. It was awful. It was the worst thing that had ever happened to me."

"What were the emotions?"

"I think I was pretty down for a while."

"How did your family handle your injury?"

Kyle said, "They were very supportive. They helped me regain perspective and understand that things could be a lot worse, that it was probably for the best."

"And how did they handle your down feelings?"

"Like I said, they helped me gain perspective."

I said, "You learned helpful realities from them, but you didn't get a lot of emotional comfort from them, at least in the sense that I am talking about."

"What do you mean?"

"I mean that while it is good to learn perspective and responsibility, it is even more important to learn to receive and be loved when we are in need or pain."

"I don't get it. They were great parents. They didn't do anything wrong. They loved me."

"Yes, I do think they did a lot of things right. But I think one problem area was that, for whatever reason, it might have been difficult for them to comfort and be with you when you weren't doing well. Perspective and responsibility are great abilities to have. But they aren't enough when we encounter losses. We need to receive emotional support from others. For example, I wonder what it would have been like for someone to tell you, 'This injury has changed a lot of your life. It's a big loss for you. I am so sorry. This is a difficult and sad time for you, and I want you to tell me what it means to you.' How would that have affected you as a teenager? Don't answer this quickly; think about it for a minute."

Kyle reflected on the question. Then gradually his face began to change and show some emotion. His eyes looked a little wet, and he said, "I don't know what is going on. I am feeling that sadness again, like when the doctor said I wouldn't be able to play anymore. I haven't had this feeling for years. What is happening to me?"

I said, "I think it probably is what should happen now."

Nancy began stirring in her seat. She watched Kyle's face closely. "You never told me this was important. Whenever we talked about your shoulder injury, you always said it was for the best, and it was a positive thing."

Kyle said, "It was for the best. I changed my college plans and I met you on campus. I would have never met you otherwise. You're the best thing that ever happened to me."

I said, "Wait, Kyle, that's true. But listen to this. Nancy never heard how you really felt about the worst thing that had ever happened to you. That loss was important for you. That part of you, that experience, brings her closer to you. And that sort of thing is what she has been missing with you."

Nancy said, "This is the closest I've felt to you in a long time."

"I don't know how to do this," Kyle said.

I said, "You're right. You just made a connection with Nancy by accident, and she responded to you. But for you to continue loving her the way that you both want, you will need to do more of this. We need to help you get more intentional and focused on letting yourself be loved."

"I don't know . . . it sounds like the opposite of what I need to do. I thought I just need to love her better."

"Sure you do, probably every husband does. But you are trying to give Nancy things you don't possess, that you haven't experienced, in a world you know little about. You are operating in a vacuum here. You want to be a *loving* husband, and you are on the way to that; you do a lot of things right. But you must be a *connected* husband for everything to work right."

"So I need to talk about my bad times in life some more?"

"Well, in a way. It's probably more accurate to say that you need to receive what it is you want to give to Nancy. I want our next few sessions to focus on you learning to open up about yourself, on a real level, with Nancy here. And I want you to begin learning to take what she offers: acceptance, safety, understanding, comfort. And let's see what happens."

Kyle and Nancy began concentrating on this. It was not easy at first, because he had always equated love with perspective and encouragement. Learning to connect on a deeper, emotional level was a new world with new rules for him. But gradually he began to be able to bring his frustrations, his failures, and his fears to Nancy. She was responsive. She loved his strength and can-do attitude, but she welcomed this other part of him.

I recommended a men's support group for Kyle, so he would have other relationships besides Nancy to open up to. He began meeting with these men and told me, "I have never talked to anyone, especially guys, at this level. This is pretty incredible."

A few weeks later, Nancy reported a breakthrough. She said, "Last night I was telling Kyle about how hard my day was with the kids and my job. Usually, he would say things like, 'I know you can make it' and 'Let me take the kids tomorrow,' which, don't get me wrong, I really appreciate, but at the same time left me feeling alone sometimes.

"But he got this emotional look on his face instead. And he said, 'Honey, sounds like this has been brutal for you. I am so sorry. Sit here and tell me what it has been like.' I could tell he really felt what he was saying. I felt a part of him, like we were in the same world, for maybe the first time."

"Great job, Kyle," I said. "What was going on inside you to make that happen?"

He said, "Nothing on purpose; maybe it was all the time opening up about myself. When Nancy started talking about how hard things were, I just got this sad feeling about how alone and powerless she must have felt, and I wanted to reach out to her and be there for her."

Kyle was making a shift in his relationship and, more importantly, within himself. He was learning to receive the connection he wanted to provide.

RECEIVING THE CONNECTION

Somewhere in the lives of all successfully loving people, there was a person or persons who reached inside and connected with them. Someone who got to the heart, who bonded. And not for some brief event or interchange, but consistently and over a period of time. Someone who got there and stayed there. The connection is what brings us the elements of what we need.

Jesus explains this in a metaphor describing his relationship with us: "Yes, I am the vine; you are the branches. Those who remain in me, and I in them, will produce much fruit. For apart from me you can do nothing. Anyone who does not remain in me is thrown away like a useless branch and withers. Such branches are gathered into a pile to be burned. But if you remain in me and my words remain in you, you may ask for anything you want, and it will be granted!"[2] This passage teaches us that just as branches cannot exist without the support and nourishment of the vine, neither can we exist without Christ. In the same way, he is showing us that no one who is disconnected from relationship, with him or his people and resources, will survive and thrive.

In addition, for years now, science has supported and illuminated the importance of attachment and connection. As we saw in the last chapter, the research shows that connected people simply have better and healthier lives.

That leads us to another point: *you need to be connected because you need it, not simply so that you will become more loving.* Connection is an important and good thing for you. God made the universe run that way. It is helpful to be clear about this. Sometimes people feel guilty about their need to be attached, as though it were selfish, demanding, or overdependent. They feel immature and worry that others will resent them. That is a common attitude of people who are more comfortable giving than receiving. They enjoy supporting, helping, and connecting with others, but asking for those things places them out of their comfort zone. So they do the output and neglect the input. They are consumed with meeting the needs of others. Then they try to minimize the receiving they experience so they refuse to bother others or put them out. Or they rationalize it, thinking, *I am just doing this because it is ultimately about helping others.*

YOU NEED TO BE CONNECTED BECAUSE YOU NEED IT, NOT SIMPLY SO THAT YOU WILL BECOME MORE LOVING.

Now, caring for others is a great thing. In fact, it ultimately has more value in the long run than being cared for. As Jesus said, "It is more blessed to give than to receive."[3] However, it is a mistake to justify your own need to be connected as simply a way to better help others. "I am only taking time to get support so that I can be a benefit to others" is not a healthy or realistic idea. It is actually based not on concern for others but comes from your own fear, guilt, and uncertainty about whether it is OK to take time and reach out for connection from yourself. You will miss the experience you need to have about how you were designed to be connected. Not only that, but you will also miss the compassion necessary to satisfy the needs of others. How will you be able to be patient, kind, and empathetic with others if you are thinking, *I'd better care about this person so she can hurry up and become a caring person also?* A person who thinks like this has an agenda in mind that has to do with the person performing in some way. Their connection to that person is not authentic; it is more of an arrangement. Whatever was going on in your interaction with that person would not be a transfer of real and true connection from you to them.

How would you feel if someone was spending time with you and you knew that he or she was involved only so you would become more giving at some point? You would feel horrible about the experience and the relationship. You would not want to really open up to that person and receive anything meaningful from him or her. You would feel like a project, a task, or an obligation. You certainly wouldn't feel desired, accepted, or valued. You are designed with a built-in need to receive good things from others. Without authentic connection, you do not do well. With it, life is better. It's as simple as that.

> WITHOUT AUTHENTIC CONNECTION, YOU DO NOT DO WELL. WITH IT, LIFE IS BETTER. SIMPLE AS THAT.

Without authentic connection, you don't do well. With it, life is better. Simple as that.

Here is an illustration of what receiving the connection might look like, based on a conversation I had recently. I hadn't seen Stan, a longtime friend, since he had moved away some time ago. When he was in town for business, he called, and we scheduled lunch. We began catching up with what was going on. The conversation took a serious turn pretty rapidly, however. Stan began to talk about a difficult period he was going through in his marriage, in which he and his wife, Alicia, were at an impasse over a recent conflict. They weren't in trouble as a couple or anything of that nature. They were, as most couples experience from time to time, going through a bad spot of feeling alienated and strained with each other.

Here is how that played out between us:

Stan: "I need to talk about Alicia and me."
Me: "What's going on?"

Stan: "It's really pretty cold between us right now. I hate how far apart we are, but she is so mad at me, I can't reconnect with her."

Me: "What happened?"

Stan: "She didn't get the promotion, and she was really upset about it. But I was pretty clueless, and I didn't realize how much that meant to her. She tried to tell me a few times, and I just didn't really pay attention. So she finally blew up."

Me: "That is tough . . . how did it go?"

Stan: "Really not a lot of fun. She got pretty harsh and said some things that yanked my chain. So I pulled away and withdrew; you know how I do that. Then I started missing her after a while. But at the same time, I don't want to trigger an explosion, so we are still just staying on the surface."

Me: "That's hard. You want the connection, but you can't pull it off."

Stan: "That's right . . . well, I know in time I'll eventually approach her again, or she'll approach me, or something. We end up doing that pretty well, you know. And each time, it gets better between us. But I feel like I'm the bad guy right now, and I'll be a worse guy if she starts raging at me."

Me: "I'm sorry things are so bad right now."

Stan: "Thanks . . . well, it helps to talk about it. I feel sane again. So I'm not the worst husband in the world?"

Me: (grinning) "Not the worst . . ."

Stan: "My buddy, thanks a lot."

And the conversation moved to other matters.

Stan and I know each other well enough to be aware that he wasn't asking for advice or guidance at that particular time. He and Alicia have been married for a long time, and they are both mature and growing individuals. He knew what the issues were, what his part was, what her part was, and what the necessary steps were to get past this. They were currently in a bad cycle, one that many couples experience, and one with clear dynamics and responsibilities. Stan was familiar with all these aspects, and in fact he knew what it would take to resolve things. All he needed from me was to understand how hard this was for him, to convey that to him, and to give him the connection he needed now. It was simply Stan's turn to receive something.

THE ESSENTIALS OF RECEIVING CONNECTION

My conversation with Stan was brief, because we have a lot of years of friendship between us. Some talks like this have to be much longer, depending on the circumstances. The important thing to notice about our conversation is that it contains the elements I am discussing in what being connected is about. Let's take a closer look at these essentials of receiving connection.

NEEDING

Stan didn't pretend to have life all together. He was feeling disconnected and troubled, and he was honest enough to admit it. He didn't waste time pretending or attempting to keep me happy. He was in a bad place with Alicia and did not like it. He knew he needed support and connection in order to do the right thing in his marriage.

Stan resisted the temptation to put his best foot forward and be positive about a negative situation. He knew that he would not receive anything good if he didn't experience his need. Being aware that you are in need is a sign of strength, not weakness. It is simply acknowledging the reality of your state, condition, or feelings. It is difficult for us to admit need sometimes, because it feels unsafe, or we may think we should be able to handle life on our own. But remember the vine and the branches metaphor we saw earlier. Branches that are on their own and cut off from the vine become brittle, dry, and dead.

Look at Stan's discomfort as an early warning signal, reminding him to talk to me at our lunch. This discomfort drove him to talk and to be vulnerable. You may have to rearrange your thinking about needs. Needs are not a curse, they are a benefit. They keep you connected to life and to others. In fact, those who do not experience needs have what psychologists call an attachment problem, and it cuts us off from warmth, care, and life itself.

Let's break down this concept of need a bit, as it is a broad concept. What

BEING AWARE
THAT YOU ARE
IN NEED IS
A SIGN OF
STRENGTH,
NOT WEAKNESS.

do we actually need to receive in our connections? Several good things:

Grace. Though often used in relation to God's care for us, *grace* is also a relational term. We are graced by God, and in turn we grace each other. The word means "undeserved favor"—that is, we need to receive favors, or all sorts of good things, from others that we have not performed for, deserved, or paid for. Grace is the sustaining force that holds the universe together. In a way, all the things we receive begin with grace; it is that profound and important. God's message to us, over and over again, is that we need "the message of his grace that is able to build you up."[4]

When people give us grace, they are being "for" us in the way that God is for us. They are on our side. You need to recognize people who have grace to give you. They are interested in you. They prove themselves to be people of character who do what they say. And they show by word, tone, eye contact, and deed that they are pulling for you. As they have been graced by God and others, they deliver it to you.

Acceptance. Acceptance is what happens when someone receives all of us in the relationship. Literally, *acceptance* means "to take to oneself." When people accept you, they can connect with all parts of you, good and bad, strong and weak, healthy and broken. They may not agree with everything about you, but they accept the reality of all of you.

Acceptance is vital to us. We will be able to connect to the extent that we are accepted. When we experience the relief that comes with letting someone know who we really are, and then accepting us, we are able to then accept ourselves. And that is critical. We cannot accept who we are unless we have been accepted by someone else first. The self-condemnation and judgment we feel blocks our acceptance, so we need to receive this from the outside. When you are around a person who seems to accept himself, you can be sure someone loving was around that person for a period of time.

For many people, acceptance was the key to learning to receive and make a connection. When they found that they could be both known and accepted at the same time, it was a breakthrough for them.

I remember Glenn, a man I saw in counseling who was in a career crisis. He was successful in the corporate world, but he did not enjoy it. He saw the corporate life as valuable and a good fit for his colleagues, but not for him. At the same time, however, he had no real direction in where he wanted to go. Over time, it became apparent that a large part of Glenn's motivation for being in the corporate environment was the urging and example of his father, who had also been extremely successful in that world. Though he was an involved and responsible dad, Glenn's father was somewhat shortsighted. Since Glenn had a good head on his shoulders, his dad assumed the corporate environment was the place for Glenn—though he did not consult with Glenn on this opinion.

In time, Glenn began to be aware that he wanted to be a teacher. He loved interacting with kids and the process of helping them learn. He got excited about retraining for this profession. But when he did, he began feeling bad about himself and that direction. A teaching career seemed inferior and not where the action of the business world was. Because of his dad's influence, Glenn began condemning his new choice even before it got a change to take off.

WE CANNOT ACCEPT WHO WE ARE UNLESS WE HAVE BEEN ACCEPTED BY SOMEONE ELSE FIRST.

I gave him an assignment: "Go to your friends in the corporate world, the ones who are really your friends, and ask them what they think of this move." He did not want to do it, because he was sure they would tell him that he was in the wrong place. But he did it, and he was amazed at their responses. They said things like: "It makes sense; I think you'll be awesome"; "What a great field to be in"; "I envy you for having the guts to go for your dream." He felt as if a weight had been lifted. He had received acceptance of his career choice from people he thought would be somewhat judging and critical. And he is now doing fine in his work as a teacher, as it truly was a good fit.

You need acceptance also. It may be for a passion or for a mistake you have made. But acceptance is one of the things you must experience when you connect with others.

Empathy. Empathy is one of our most basic needs. It is an emotional aspect of relationship. It has to do with allowing another person to *feel with us*, to feel what we are feeling. If you are sad, the person feels sad along with you. If you are happy, the person feels happy with you also. They are not actually feeling your feelings; your feelings are yours and theirs are theirs. But they are experiencing their version of the emotions you feel. Empathy is a way of identifying with the experience of someone else, not on an intellectual level but an emotional one.

EMPATHY BRINGS US OUT OF OUR ESSENTIAL ISOLATION AND INTO THE WORLD OF RELATIONSHIP, CONNECTION, FRIENDSHIP, AND LIFE ITSELF.

Why is empathy significant? Empathy is concerned with feelings and is the reason we have feelings in the first place. Emotions are a signal to others of how we are doing so that we know how to treat one another. Feelings connect us to one another. When you are angry at someone, you want to confront the person to stop some danger. When you are anxious, you want to avoid someone because you are afraid of some response. When you feel love toward someone, you want to move toward them to become closer.

Empathy brings us out of our essential isolation and into the world of relationship, connection, friendship, and life itself. It drives us and equips to love each other. When you have empathy for someone, you want to figure out a way to help that person.

For example, I was at one of my son's football games last season. It was a tight game, with no clear winner by the last quarter. My son was in a play in which he didn't execute well. This ended up being a factor in his team losing the game. When I talked to my son later about the game, his deep discouragement and sadness were written all over his face. He felt worthless over letting down his teammates. As we sat and I listened, I began to feel also discouraged and sad, as if I were going through it. I did not try to make these feelings exist, in order to help my son. They just appeared, triggered by love and connection. The presence of those feelings helped me to be with him and simply let him talk. He did not leave the conversation cheered up. But he left knowing he was not alone with his disappointment.

Empathy is something that only comes from being empathized with. You cannot manufacture empathy. Only when another person has been attuned to your emotional state, and responded to you by feeling their similar emotions, can you develop the capacity for empathy. Empathy, as all these capacities, must be received before it can be given.

The primary source for empathy for all of us is our parents, especially our mother. As a mother experiences her infant's feelings, the baby can then be connected, safe, and loved. This is why children whose mothers are depressed, emotionally unavailable, or devoid of empathy are often cut off and detached kids. They need to find other, more accessible sources of empathy to finish the work that was interrupted in them. Ultimately, the final source of all empathy is God. His empathy for our isolation, hurts, and failures enters us, through himself directly and through his people. His supply of empathy is inexhaustible, as the psalmist expresses: "You have collected all my tears in your bottle."[5] Empathy is clearly tied to receiving. As you are empathized with, so you can empathize.

EMPATHY, AS ALL THESE CAPACITIES, MUST BE RECEIVED BEFORE IT CAN BE GIVEN.

Empathy is clearly tied to receiving. As you are empathized with, so you can empathize.

One of the first indicators that people may have some deficit in receiving empathy is that they do not experience emotional identification when others hurt. They may help and assist when someone is sad, afraid, or hurt, and they may even feel sympathy, but they do not have the corresponding feelings for others that show the presence of empathy. If you find this in yourself, it may be a sign that you need to experience another person feeling your feelings, especially negative and painful ones, in order to bring you into connection and life.

Validation. We all need to have our experiences and our feelings validated by others. To validate is to attribute reality and seriousness to something or someone. *Validation* comes from the term *valid,* meaning "grounded and meaningful." So when someone validates your experiences, they are saying, in effect, "What you are saying and feeling is real, and I'm taking it seriously, because I take you seriously." They are, in effect, placing a "validation stamp" on your feelings, in the same way that a judge validates a contract between two parties. As the agreement is now a binding reality, so your experience is a reality that makes a difference to the other person.

For example, I was working with a couple, Rich and Cindy, who were struggling in their marriage. Rich tended to be somewhat impulsive, especially when he felt threatened or unsafe. He would say angry things to Cindy that he really did not mean, but which bothered her. On her part, Cindy would underreact to Rich and would say, "There you go again with the drama." So they were alienated from each other, and it was not getting better.

EMPATHY IS CLEARLY TIED TO RECEIVING. AS YOU ARE EMPATHIZED WITH, SO YOU CAN EMPATHIZE.

In most marriage counseling, there is a shift as time goes on in which the work becomes more effective. During the first few sessions, the couple talks about the conflicts they are having at home in theory, as an abstraction. The therapist tries to understand the issue but is not seeing it. Then, when the couple feels more relaxed and safe in the counseling, they bring the conflict to the session. This is not intentional. It is simply that they begin relating at the counseling office the way they relate at home. And this makes the counseling work much more powerful, for the therapist is now actually experiencing the problem as it is happening in the room.

That is what happened eventually with Rich and Cindy. They were talking about Rich's mother, whom Cindy felt was too involved in the marriage. She thought Rich preferred his mother over her, and actually I agreed with Cindy—he hadn't really cut the cord yet. It had been a sore spot between them for a long time. She told Rich, "Sometimes it feels like you're more married to her than you are to me."

Rich reacted angrily. He said, "So you're saying I'm a little boy and not a good husband. I am never good enough for you."

Cindy's response was, "You just don't get it. You're overreacting, and you're going to make this about me again, not about you."

Rich began to ramp up in anger. I interrupted and said, "Wait a minute. Cindy, I want you to try something."

"What?" she said.

"Look at Rich in the eyes and say, 'Do you really feel that way, like you're not good enough for me?'"

"He knows that's not true," she said.

I said, "I'm not sure about that. But you will not get anywhere you want to go until you do this and mean it. I think he really does feel that way, and I want you to think how you would feel if you thought you weren't good enough for Rich."

Cindy's face softened as she turned the tables in her mind. Finally she said, "Do you really feel you're not good enough for me?"

Rich was still mad. "Of course; you make me feel that way all the time. That's what I've been trying to tell you."

I kept coaching Cindy. "Tell him how difficult that must be to have to carry that around."

Cindy said, "I had no idea you felt that way. I guess I didn't take it seriously when you said it. That must be awful to feel that I can't be pleased by you."

"Yes, it is awful," Rich said, becoming calmer and more connected. "I hate it, and I feel like I'll never measure up."

I interjected, "You don't sound as angry, Rich."

"I'm angry, but it's not as bad."

I said, "You sound a little sad."

He thought for a moment. "I think so. I guess I just want Cindy to think well of me. I know I screw up a lot, and she's right about this thing with my mom. But when I have feelings about our differences, it's always about how defensive I am."

I said, "I'm glad you can see that she's right about the mom thing. We'll get to that. But first I want to point something out to you, Cindy. Right or wrong, Rich's feelings need to be validated, unless he is attacking or being really mean to you, and I haven't seen that in him."

Cindy said, "No, he's not like that."

I said, "Well, he just needs to know that you see his feelings as real and important, and I think he'll be able to move on from there to the issue at hand. But what you do instead is dismiss and negate his experience."

She frowned. "No, I don't."

I said, "You just did it to me! As soon as I said something that doesn't make sense in your world, you immediately said it wasn't true. That is dismissing and negating, and it cuts people off from you, especially Rich."

Cindy was a quick study, and she caught on. "Yes, I do tend to correct what I think are his misperceptions."

"And that is fine at the right time. But when he is having strong feelings, it's the wrong time. I want you to learn what I had you do a few minutes ago, with validating his feelings of not being good enough for you. I want you to be able to do this in lots of contexts in your marriage, from finances to sex to parenting to in-laws. And Rich, I want you to learn to also validate Cindy's feelings. It is a two-way street."

Cindy was not giving up without a fight. "But this is just agreeing with him, even when he is wrong."

"I know you think that, but that is not what is going on. When you validate someone and let him know his feelings are real and important, you aren't agreeing with what the feelings are saying. You are just saying that you don't take his feelings lightly. If Rich says he's so mad he'll quit his job, and you say, 'You must be really angry right now,' you're not saying, 'I know you're going to quit, and I agree with you—go for it!' You're just letting him know that he must be really upset to make such a rash statement."

Cindy began to work on validating Rich more, instead of negating his experience. At first she thought she was babying him and giving in to him. But what she noticed is that he would calm down sooner, admit when he was wrong, and then want to find out her side of things also. He became more caring with Cindy and a better listener.

In time, Rich's overreactions had resolved, and he was able to handle stress, correction, confrontation, and failure in a more adult fashion. And Cindy felt more like they were relating as mutual equals, not as the grown-up and the emotional kid. But it started when she began to validate.

You need someone to validate your experience *the way you experience and feel it, not necessarily from objective reality.* That connects us to others. It also helps us feel that our experience matters, helps us to feel real ourselves, and then helps us move on to what the real truth and reality is. Nothing can disconnect and shut us down quicker than to take a risk and tell a person something from our heart, only to be told, "That's not how you really feel" or "That's not right." Our feelings are our feelings. We need to know those emotions matter and are serious business to someone. The connection must include validation of your experience, right or wrong at the time.

Understanding. We need for someone to "get it" about us. Everyone needs to be understood. By understanding, I mean we need another person to make sense of the realities, facts, and truths of our life. When you seek to be understood, it has more to do with objective realities than emotional ones.

Understanding involves not only literally understanding a person's language but also understanding the deeper issues and motives. When we say that someone "gets it about me," we are talking about the experience of that person seeing who we really are inside. It is as if the person is saying, "What you are saying makes sense." When we feel as though they don't "get us," we are saying that even though they may understand the surface, they don't truly comprehend what we are experiencing.

For example, Brett, a single man I was counseling, was a classic commitmentphobe. He had a pattern of pursuing a woman, and then, when the relationship got too close for him, he would withdraw or somehow end the relationship. Basically, the loving feelings he was experiencing would disappear. It was hard on the women, especially Kathy, his most recent girlfriend and the one whom he had been able to become the most connected to. They had had more times of vulnerability and intimacy than he had ever had, which was progress. At the same time, it was very difficult for Kathy when they were on the verge of breaking up. She was hurt and angry.

Brett asked if I could see them together to see if there was any hope to work out the conflict. When we met, Kathy talked about how upset she was about Brett's withdrawal from her.

> YOU NEED SOMEONE TO VALIDATE YOUR EXPERIENCE THE WAY YOU EXPERIENCE AND FEEL IT, NOT NECESSARILY FROM OBJECTIVE REALITY.

"I really cared about you," she said. "And I let you inside and allowed myself to think that maybe we had a future together. And now it looks like that was foolish of me."

Brett felt very bad about what was happening. He said, "I know I am doing this, and I don't want to. You certainly don't deserve this. I just don't feel anymore what I wanted to feel about us, and you haven't changed; it's me."

I asked Kathy, "Do you understand why Brett is losing his feelings for you?"

She said, "I don't know. Maybe he is playing a game with me. Or maybe he never cared. Or maybe he wants me to be someone I can't be."

Brett protested, "No, none of that is true, Kathy! I really do want to feel closer to you, but I just can't."

I said, "Kathy, I believe that Brett hasn't lost his feelings for you for another reason. I agree with Brett that it's not a game or some deception. He truly cares about you and who you are as a person, but he is also truly stuck.

"Here is what I think. Brett, you have a pattern of getting close and then feeling nothing with women you date. And as we know, you've gotten closer to Kathy than anyone else, but it still happened. From what you report to me about these relationships, it seems that your emotions are going away with Kathy not because anything is wrong with her, but the opposite, because *so much is right about her.* That is, her character qualities, her values, her love for you, and her interests all are very attractive to you. And I think you are just scared that you might lose control and fall in love with her."

"What is wrong with that? That is what I want to happen."

"There's nothing wrong with falling in love; it's a great thing. But at the same time, you are afraid that if you allow yourself to need someone that much and want her to know you that deeply, you will be so vulnerable and exposed that it will be too much of a risk to take. If you let Kathy in all the way, she would, in your mind, have tremendous power to ruin you if she chose to leave the relationship."

Brett was quiet. Finally he said, "I think that is true. That fits all the other dating relationship problems I have had, at least the ones that mattered to me."

I continued. "The reality is, however, that even if that happens, you won't be ruined or destroyed. It might hurt, but you would be able to recover and move on. It's just an old fear from a long time ago, and you can resolve this."

Kathy said, "Are you saying we might be able to go on? I'm not sure I want to go through the roller coaster. This is hard for me."

I said, "I totally understand, Kathy. But if you could take a little time to let Brett process this reality, it might help." Kathy agreed.

The next session, Brett came alone. He said, "I have been thinking about this fear. Now that I know more, and it's not that I'm crazy or a bad guy, I am feeling more emotions for Kathy. It seems safer, and I want to be with her."

Kathy was patient, and Brett in a fairly short period of time regained his feelings for her. He was able to take the risk of being close to her, and their relationship deepened.

The point is this: Brett needed someone to understand why he was doing something that seemed so illogical—even mean. Kathy was bewildered. Brett himself was confused. But we had worked together long enough that I had seen the pattern. And that helped to again release the loving feelings he had for her. We all need someone to understand what is going on underneath the surface that drives and influences our behavior.

We all need to be understood. None of us can totally understand why we do what we do, because we are too close to ourselves. When someone steps in from the outside and helps shine an insight or a clarification on our world, things begin to make sense. And further than that, we experience again what it is like to be connected. Actually, there is some overlap between understanding in connection and the aspect of truth-telling, the next element of being a loving person. The difference between the two is that understanding has more to do with experiencing that the other person sees us as we really are and illuminates things for us; truth-telling is more about the experience of how confrontation is part of love. But the two are related.

WE ALL NEED TO BE UNDERSTOOD.

Most of us can relate to one or more of these needs: grace, empathy, acceptance, validation, and understanding. If you discover that you have some lack in these areas, it is a good idea to find people who have what you possess. Think about your present friends and relationships. Are there individuals who seem to have these qualities that you need? If so, in the next section, we will go over how to use those connections to help you become a loved person. If these types of people are not around, you will need to take some steps to find them. You might seek out a church that promotes relationships and ask if there are people or groups who work with these matters. You can also find out if there are therapists in the community who are experienced in helping people with these needs. They generally are glad to be involved, for they see the value of the process.

ASKING

My out-of-town friend, Stan, whom we met earlier in this chapter, took the next step. He brought his need for support to the relationship, taking initiative to ask for some time for us to talk about his situation. That was the only way I would have known about the conflict in his marriage. Our conversation took some effort and some humility. We all have to fight the demons of being afraid the other person will see us as weak or judge us. But that is the work of receiving. There really is no shortcut here. People who ask for love and support do not get what they need every single time. But those who do not ask are far less likely. It is the same with us and God: "You do not have, because you do not ask God."[6] Asking is a requirement for connecting.

When you put yourself in the position of asking, those who are truly on your team will be happy to fulfill your request. When we care about someone, it does us good to know that we are valuable to them, especially in such a vulnerable area. We were designed so that life works better when we are both connected and connecting. So realize that you are most likely benefiting others when you ask; you are not putting them out or draining them.

I hit a writer's block when working on this book. The ideas would not come. Businesspeople, athletes, musicians, pastors, and anyone trying to create something commonly experience this problem. Even though I have written a good number of books, this had never happened to me. I had often heard about it from other writers but had never personally experienced it. It was terrible. I found myself avoiding writing, doing other tasks instead, such as answering e-mails and phone calls that could wait. But I could not make myself write. I'm sure that part of the reason was that love is a noteworthy subject, and I was concerned about getting my arms around something so important and so broad. But nothing worked.

Finally, I was talking to a friend, Jeremy, about the dilemma. Time was moving on, and I was behind on the book. I was getting nervous. We talked for a while about the problem and my attempts to break out of the block. As we were talking, an idea occurred to me. I told Jeremy, "I wonder if it would help to just call someone for a couple of minutes every day and read what I have written to him. That might be a structure to help me be accountable to do something every day and get engaged in the writing process on a regular basis."

Jeremy said, "That makes sense to me."

Then he questioned me. "Are you asking me to do this with you?"

I was embarrassed. "No, no, no way," I said. "Every day is a lot of commitment, and it's probably not a good idea for a friend to do it. I can probably outsource this, maybe pay someone to do it; that makes more sense."

"OK, you pay someone. Would that motivate you to get something written if you paid them?"

I thought about it. "I guess not," I said. "I would just figure, I'm paying for their time, and whether or not I call, they get the money. So it wouldn't matter. It probably wouldn't work."

Jeremy said, "So quit beating around the bush. Are you asking me or not?"

"I guess I am."

He kept pushing. "That's not asking."

I was really squirming by now. The prospect of asking a friend to put himself out for me was very uncomfortable. But he knew, and I knew, I had to ask. "OK, can I call you every day for a few minutes and read what I have written?"

"Yes. Why don't we go over our calendars and get things scheduled?"

The plan worked. For about a month, I called him daily. I had to daily fight the guilt and the sense of imposing on Jeremy. But more importantly, the words began to come, because I had to have something to talk about! And the block gradually resolved. But the point to be made here is that even if it causes discomfort, and it often does, connected people get connected by asking. It does not happen by wishing, hoping, and waiting for others to recognize the need and respond.

Probably the only exception to this is the first few months of life, when infants need for their mother to read their reactions and needs and tend to them with warmth, care, and nurture. Newborns are not developed enough to take that sort of responsibility. So mothers take the initiative, until the baby has internalized enough safety and care to be able to begin gradually taking more and more ownership over the process of asking. And a baby's cry is simply a form of asking. So even from birth, we are designed to be people who ask.

You may be afraid or embarrassed to ask. You may have problems trusting others. Or you may not have much experience with asking. That happens often in significant relationships and in families of origin. So your task might be to tell someone safe who has the love to offer that you have a hard time asking. You want them to help you do this. You need them, in a word, to help you ask to ask! We all know what a risk asking is. But take the step with these people. It is worth it.

TAKING IT IN

Becoming connected involves a transfer. Something real and actual changes hands, or in this case, hearts. You need grace, acceptance, validation, or some other element of a good attachment. Someone, like Jeremy, offers it and transfers it to you for your use and benefit. It is yours to enjoy and grow from, as it is transferred from one person to the other.

You must receive the connection in order to make the transfer complete. Just as when you do an online transfer of funds from one bank account to another, the transfer is not finished until the account being funded actually has the money in it.

So you must take in what is offered. It is not enough to simply be in the presence of the person caring about you. A person can have all sorts of accepting and validating thoughts and feelings toward you. He can tell you, by word, body language, and deeds how much he values you. But it takes receiving for you to finish the job!

Let's explain exactly what taking someone inside is. Technically, it means to come into possession of something, as in the financial sense just described. You own and can control whatever form of connection has been given to you. In the world of love and relationships, the best way to come into possession of the care that another has for you is *to allow yourself to experience what is being offered.* You are putting yourself in a position to feel and truly know the reality of what the person wants you to have for yourself. There is something good here. The need you have meets, comes into contact with, and takes in whatever element of attachment the person provides.

> YOU MUST RECEIVE THE CONNECTION IN ORDER TO MAKE THE TRANSFER COMPLETE.

Think about a time when you greeted a loved one you had not seen for a while—at a restaurant or a home, or an airport. Most of us will hug that person, look at her face, and tell her how glad we are to see her again. Longing, desire, and need are replaced by joy, happiness, and satisfaction. We are experiencing their presence and letting it come into us. Our need connects with the person, and that is all receiving really is.

Wholeheartedness. You need to learn to get over your hesitation and reservation, and engage in the relationship. Look at that person's eyes. Listen attentively to what she is saying to you. Open your heart and your emotions to what she wants to give you. Give the person your full attention. Feel the need for grace or understanding while you are with her. Enjoy it, appreciate it, and be grateful for it. Be expectant. Something good is coming your way! It's good for the other person, and it's good for you. God created life to work that way, in both directions. Jesus said, "Give as freely as you have received,"[7] which assumes you have received freely.

To become a loving person, you have to take in the connection. And you cannot be ambivalent about it. Many people have trouble receiving wholeheartedly because they do not want to appear selfish or demanding. This is a real problem. It is confusing needs with selfishness. They are not the same thing and need to be seen as very different. When our needs are met, we grow, mature, heal, and give back in gratitude. When our selfishness is met, we get more immature, sicker, and more self-centered. This is a big contrast.

When our sons sit down to dinner after sports in the afternoon, often the first few minutes of the meal are quiet. My wife and I have a few minutes to ourselves at the table while the boys are busily engaged in pounding massive amounts of food and liquid into their depleted systems. They chew, drink, swallow, and do it over and over and over again. They are wholeheartedly receiving. It is an amazing thing to observe. I wish my body would allow me to eat like that without gaining a hundred pounds!

Then, after a while, they look up and start talking with us about the day. They enter the family atmosphere and connect. Their pressing need has been met,

IN THE WORLD OF LOVE AND RELATIONSHIPS, THE BEST WAY TO COME INTO POSSESSION OF THE CARE THAT ANOTHER HAS FOR YOU IS TO ALLOW YOURSELF TO EXPERIENCE WHAT IS BEING OFFERED.

and they are ready to be with us. It would be absurd to say, "You are so selfish; remember that it's not all about you." The reality is, when you are in great need, it is all about you for the moment, and you had better pay attention to your need. If you miss the opportunity, you may not get what should come your way, and you could harm yourself. Pay attention to your desire and need, and allow the good to enter.

Some people don't receive wholeheartedly because they are afraid. They have had painful experiences with relationship, and they are anxious that the love they want will then be removed or withdrawn. Then they would be worse off than if they had never opened up in the first place. So they avoid receiving, or at least receiving wholeheartedly. They can be timid, hesitant, and reserved in receiving. This can certainly be a reality, but you must deal with this and resolve it. Find safe people who care. Take risks. Open up as best you can. Make little steps of progress over and over again. Over time, most people can learn to heal their fears of receiving.

> **TO BECOME A LOVING PERSON, YOU HAVE TO TAKE IN THE CONNECTION. AND YOU CANNOT BE AMBIVALENT ABOUT IT.**

When I am working with a couple having a hard time connecting, sometimes it is because one is not able to wholeheartedly receive compassion or empathy from the other. There is fear, guilt or a host of problems preventing the transfer. I will often have them face each other and look into each other's eyes while one offers something loving to the other. And I will instruct the one receiving, "Listen to what he is saying right now. Don't pay attention to anything but what he is offering, and how much you need what he is offering." Sometimes they will have a breakthrough as they focus, often for the first time, on the act of receiving well and wholeheartedly. They will feel alive inside, or get a spark of hope, or become full, or sometimes break into tears. Receiving is a blessing, and it needs to happen.

Here is a way to make receiving happen for you. Tell the people you are learning to ask for love from that you need help hanging in there when they respond. Let them know, "I tend to avoid letting someone in, and sometimes

I break eye contact, change the subject, or think that you are just being nice." Help them to be a team member, and keep them informed. They can hold you accountable to the process and, when you avoid things, say, "I think you just moved away. Are you still here?" This is good feedback and a helpful process.

USING

Needing, asking, and receiving are not the complete picture in connecting. We need to *use* what is given to us. Connection has a purpose. It is not meant to be stagnant any more than gasoline was meant to be siphoned into a car that just sits there, never starting up and driving away. Connection fuels your life. It is active, and it requires activity so that it can be useful and helpful in life. Connected people are people who are grateful for what they have taken in and do not want to waste it. They want to burn the gasoline to go places in life that are important to them.

Sometimes we just use our connections to survive and keep going. Remember, connection is not a luxury; it is a necessity, a requirement for life. You may need to get your daily minimum just to make it for another day, and that is good. You probably need more to get further along than survival, but you certainly need that.

But when we do use our connections, good things happen. Husbands feel like less of a failure, people take career risks that are fulfilling, kids move on from a sports defeat, wives move toward their husbands, single people resolve fears, and books get written. Connection requires movement and response from us when we experience it. The receiver has a responsibility for what he receives; he is accountable. Connection takes time and energy from someone you care about, even if it is freely given. That is not a guilt motive; it is a reality motive. Take ownership over connecting with others, and help it help you to be a better and more whole person.

> CONNECTED PEOPLE ARE PEOPLE WHO ARE GRATEFUL FOR WHAT THEY HAVE TAKEN IN AND DO NOT WANT TO WASTE IT.

THE DISCONNECTED STATE

This next section is very important, especially if connection has not worked well for you in life. There is a difference between having a normal need to receive connection from others and being in a disconnected state. They are not the same thing, and we should deal with them in different ways as well.

In normal life, we all need to regularly receive the good from caring people around us. Like taking a daily multivitamin, we make sure that we are in frequent contact with individuals who care and want to connect with us. That is what lunches with friends, phone calls, small group settings, and other contexts are about. There is no specific problem or need beyond the reality that people care about each other and want to spend time together. Issues come up, joys are celebrated, problems are empathized with, solutions are suggested, griefs are shared. In other words, connection never ends. It is a practice that continues for your lifetime. It adds meaning, purpose, and joy to our days.

The state of disconnection is different. Disconnection is not a lonely few hours or a couple of days when we miss a loved one. It is something static and unchanging, whether or not people are around us. *Disconnection is the inability to feel and experience the warmth of connection over time.* It is the absence of the security of being attached. It is the lack of bonding inside. People who are disconnected do not feel connected, understood, or valued. This can be acutely painful or deeply lonely, often with a sense of abandonment or feeling as though one is a bad, worthless person. Sometimes it is simply the experience of not feeling alive inside or not having any emotions.

> DISCONNECTION IS THE INABILITY TO FEEL AND EXPERIENCE THE WARMTH OF CONNECTION OVER TIME.

We were not designed to exist in a disconnected state. We were meant to be able to sustain and keep a sense of being loved, *even when alone.* That is one way we know if we are in an unloved state: do we still feel connected and cared about when no one is around?

To be alone does not also mean to be lonely. If we are in a loved state, it means we are drawing on the love and grace that we have received from others over time—many, many experiences from one or several significant people. When we are by ourselves, feeling stressful, having difficulties or other negative experiences, love comforts and stabilizes us.

How do we reach a connected state? The process by which we take in and use the attachment we have received in becoming a loved person is called *internalization.* The word literally means we place inside of ourselves the emotional experiences of care that come to us from others. Every time you receive from others, an emotional memory of that transaction comes to rest inside you. Eventually, these build up over time within you. Finally, there are enough of these supportive, accepting, and positive memories amassed that you shift from being in an isolated or disconnected state to a connected one. It becomes a constant and permanent part of you. The Bible describes one of the aspects of spiritual growth as being "rooted and grounded in love."[8] This is a good picture of how internalization brings to us a solid, consistent state of being connected.

Emotional memories are different from the memories we have of events in our lives. Everyday memories are mental recordings we make of what goes on: trips, parties, meetings, work activities, and so on. They serve as a journal of what has happened to us over the years. Emotional memories are much more personal. They carry with them the feelings that we received from someone and also the emotions we felt toward that person. They are highly charged.

An example of an emotional memory might be a time you had a bad problem in a love relationship, and you talked to a safe and compassionate friend about it. She was empathic and understanding, and you felt those realities. Not only that, but you carried that memory with you and probably can still feel what it was like talking to her, though it may have occurred some time back. You internalized a loving emotional memory, and memories such as these are very valuable and useful to us. We need lots of them.

This internalization process first occurs in infancy and early childhood. It is one of the most

TO BE ALONE DOES NOT ALSO MEAN TO BE LONELY. IF WE ARE IN A LOVED STATE, IT MEANS WE ARE DRAWING ON THE LOVE AND GRACE THAT WE HAVE RECEIVED FROM OTHERS OVER TIME.

important tasks of these years. You see, babies do not come out of the womb in a bonded and connected state. They are instead terrified, confused, unstable, and feeling desperately alone. Babies are born crying and wailing, with painful expressions on their faces. That is the nature of the birth process.

One of the very first things a mother does with her newborn, then, is to begin to undo that problem. She reaches out to him, holds him close, and warms him with her body. It is her way of saying, "Welcome, you are loved and safe" to her child, and it begins the process of his internalization.

On his part, the baby is busy also. He is performing the tasks I have described that we must all do to become an attached person: needing (feeling alone and afraid), asking (signaling to his mother by crying), receiving (taking in his mother's love and warmth), and using (being able to calm down and become stable). So from the very beginning of life, the pattern is established that we are to follow until the end of life: taking in the good from the outside.

The process continues, with the baby and his mom continuing the internalization process until the point, typically at around three years old or so, he feels secure because she has "been there" for him enough and consistently that he can be OK for a while when she is not around, because he has the emotional memories of her to sustain him. He has developed a bonded and connected state inside. At this point, he takes more risks to scoot away from her and practice his own independence for short periods of time, in the "trying three-year-old" period. But there is no way he could feel safe enough to run to another aisle in the grocery store and hide from his mom unless he had the loved state as his foundation and safety net.

The entire process is a little like charging your cell phone battery. When you plug the adaptor cord into the wall outlet, you need to leave it in for a few hours before it is ready to go for an entire day. If you disconnect it too soon, it will fail before it is supposed to. In the same way, the internalization process must be constant and good over time, until its work has been completed and a connected person in a connected state is the result.

Unfortunately, this is not often the case. The battery charge is interrupted too soon, in many ways. Sometimes a mother is not as emotionally available as she needs to be for her baby and doesn't provide a lot of empathy, compassion, and grace for him. Sometimes she has her own struggles and crises that pull her away. Sometimes she has her own character issues, and is inconsistent, alternating randomly between love and anger or withdrawal. Sometimes she becomes dependent on her baby, intruding on him and smothering him emotionally rather than caring for him based on his own needs. Sometimes there is trauma or loss that detracts from the process.

This does not always mean that the person will not be able to be connected. Sometimes the child or youth will have a relationship with another person, not the mother, whose warmth and care can accomplish a great deal to continue the process. I have known people who were fortunate enough to have a very loving father, aunt, neighbor, grandmother, and so on, and that person did, over time, provide the needed grace, validation, and care. We often can supplement in better relationships what we did not experience in other ones.

However, many people do still end up in adulthood without the benefit of the connected state. And it can cause problems in relationships, behavior, and work. People who aren't connected can pick out the wrong people to love, they can develop depressions and addictions, and they can experience frustrations in achieving their career goals. The lack of a foundation of internalized attachment keeps them off balance, fearful, untrusting, or too dependent. That is why this state is so vital to us.

YOU CAN BECOME THE CONNECTED PERSON YOU WERE MEANT TO BE.

If you identify the disconnected state as something you experience, the situation is not hopeless, and you do not have to resign yourself to be in this position permanently. The good news is that adults can finish the attachment process that did not get finished in childhood. You do not have to live out your life feeling alone or disconnected. You can receive and store up good, healthy, validating experiences with others that can complete the battery charge, so to speak. It happens all the time and is part of the restorative and redemptive process that God designed for us. He has not left you, to be alone inside yourself. He has set up a process in which you can regain what was lost: "I will repay you for the years the locusts have eaten."[9]

The process uses the elements I described earlier: needing, asking, receiving, and using. The attachment process is the same for all of us, no matter how young or old we are. You need to find safe people who will invest in your life and help you finish the job and repair what might have been injured inside.

You need to be in this process with them over a period of time. It requires some stability and an attachment to these people. It can't be done with quick changes of people. Internalizing what we need means that we take risks with the people who are with us, and we need to see that they are with us and will be with us. But they are out there, in healthy churches, small groups, counseling contexts, and good friendships. You can become the connected person you were meant to be. Your future does not have to be a continuation of your past. It can be a different and much better way of living.

Some disconnected states are mild, some are moderate, and some are severe, depending on the circumstances, the individual's responses, and the resources available to him. Generally speaking, a person who can feel and experience the need for connection and love, but still feels unloved or has difficulty trusting or opening up to others, has had to undergo less severe injury. On the other hand, some people feel little or no need or longing for personal closeness with others. They would like to be loved and connected, and they understand the importance intellectually. But they cannot experience the need inside. These people are dealing with *detachment*, which is an emotional disconnectedness. They need to work on being able to become safe enough with the right people. Eventually, they should be able to feel the needs and longings inside that have been cut off and denied access to. That then prepares them to be able to receive the warmth and bonding they need in order to develop a lasting connected state.

A TRANSFORMATION

I have known many people who discovered they lived in the disconnected state, realized that was the source of a lot of their problems, and then went through the process of connection and attaching successfully. They are now doing fine in life as connected people, and they can keep good relationships and have very meaningful lives. One example is Mallory, a former client.

Mallory was a married working mother in her mid-thirties. She came to me for counseling to deal with some mild depression and communication problems with her husband. What we discovered rather quickly was that Mallory was operating in life from a disconnected state. She wanted closeness and contact with others, and saw it as important. Yet she tended to avoid opening up to others and letting them know how she really felt about things in her heart. She couldn't need or let herself receive. She loved her husband, family, and friends. But she could not experience them loving her back. And of course, this contributed to the depression and marriage issue.

Mallory's pattern was that she would give support and care to others in her life, providing warmth and friendship, and it was authentic. But no one really knew her desires, hurts, negative feelings, and loneliness. And since she was not only caring but also smart and very capable, her lack of attachment was not readily apparent. She was active in the community, a leader in the church and in her job.

Mallory's caring nature and her high level of functioning effectively masked the deep disconnection she felt inside. People thought she was fine, and she seemed happy. She was not being deceptive or manipulative; she was doing the best she could. She lived out an irony: she was surrounded by people and yet did not feel a part of anyone.

Mallory was aware of some of this. She would say, "I know that I know a lot more about people than they do about me. But honestly, it is easier for me this way. I feel that it would be inappropriate for me to burden others with my problems and feelings. People have their own struggles; they don't need to deal with mine also. Besides, I am not sure it would go well if I did let myself need someone. That has been painful at other times in life."

Mallory was referring to a childhood in which her mother was quite needy and overwhelmed with life. Her father, though he cared for Mallory, worked a lot and was emotionally distant. So she learned quickly that to need, ask, or try to receive compassion or validation from her mom would result in her mother feeling more overwhelmed and like a martyr: "After all I am going through, you want to give me more to deal with?" And her dad just could not communicate on an emotional level, though he tried to spend time with her and do activities with her.

Mallory's solution to this family environment was to learn to mother her mother. She developed the ability to read her mom's moods and learned how to listen to her, support her, and calm her down. Most of all, she learned how not to be a burden to her. Rather than go through the normal childhood experiences of receiving her mom's grace, compassion, and validation for all the seasons of being a little girl, she lived in a world in which she was the mature one who quietly made sure her mom was glued together.

This pattern continued throughout her life and, as usually happens, repeated itself in her marriage and other friendships. Mallory found herself gravitating toward needy, self-absorbed people, as well as distant, unavailable individuals. So she created a relational world which mirrored and supported her internal unloved world: a world in which she would provide but would not be provided for.

In addition, Mallory noticed that she often did not have the emotional resources to give to others the way she thought they needed them—and the way she wanted to. She would find herself not wanting to be with people, or when she was with them, losing concentration on what they were saying or even feeling resentful of their needs. As we have seen, we cannot give what we do not have. She was hitting the bottom of the tank of her resources to help others.

During one session, I told her, "We have discussed and now understand where a lot of this disconnected state in you comes from. It says a lot about your character that you have done so well this far in life. But you are going to have to make some changes to repair and grow in the ways that will help you."

Mallory said, "What changes are you talking about?"

I said, "You are going to have to become comfortable needing, asking, and receiving emotional support from others."

She said, "I can learn to do that, but I will never become comfortable or really OK with it. It feels too selfish and risky."

I said, "That is a problem. Until you deal with these fears, you will not be able to make connection a normal and good part of your life. And you won't get the life results you want. We need for you to face these fears and resolve them so you can enter the world of connection the right way, not just as the giver."

Mallory worked hard on this in our sessions. She also joined a small group that had some warm people who helped her begin to open up about herself and her needs. It was difficult for her, especially at first. She had to deal with memories of worrying that she was responsible for others' happiness, as she had been for her mother. She had to recognize how lonely and isolated she had been and how empty she felt inside, with nowhere to go. And she had to take responsibility for her habit of turning conversations back to other people and their situations so that she would not have to risk asking for empathy and grace.

But after a while, Mallory was learning that there were people who really wanted to give her understanding and would not become overwhelmed or turn the conversation back to themselves. She began to allow them to get to know her world, her needs, and her desires. It took many repetitions of connecting with people on the receiving end. It took confronting her tendencies to dismiss the importance of her needs. And it took making her aware of how she did not give her friends credit for caring about her but would assume they did not want to hear how she was. And gradually, she entered the life of the connected state. She is still an involved, caring person, but her depression resolved and her marriage has improved greatly.

Something else happened inside Mallory when she truly became a connected person. Her loving nature transformed into something even better. Her depth of ability to care, empathize, and validate others increased in quality and quantity. She found she was able to connect on a deeper and more helpful level with others. And she was also able to be there with individuals for longer periods of time without feeling drained and empty. She was truly able to comfort to the level that she had been comforted, much like the principle the Bible teaches about how we are to receive and give care from God: "Who comforts us in all our troubles, so that we can comfort those in any trouble with the comfort we ourselves have received from God."[10]

You may be able to relate to Mallory. I have seen businessmen, teenagers, leaders, pastors, singles, and married people become transformed into connected people by entering this process of growth. Find a setting, such as an inviting church, competent therapist, and relationally based small group, where people know how this process works, and get involved. The growth process works, and finding true connection is worth it.

Here is a personal example of how the connected state works for us in life. Recently, one of my teenage sons finished all the requirements to prepare him to take the Department of Motor Vehicles driving permit test. He had done a lot of work to get to this point, and he was very focused and intent on passing the test. If you remember your own adolescence, you know that there is almost nothing more important about the teenage years than being able to drive. A driver's license symbolizes independence, freedom, power, and maturity during that stage of life. My son was very ready to get on with this step.

We made plans for me to drive him to the DMV. It was a fairly tight schedule, with school, sports, and work. And this was the only day I could do it that week because of how long things take at the DMV. We only had this window of time. But my son had studied, and we had both carved out the time. I drove home early from work, picked him up, and took him on the road. On the way, I took a wrong turn. I corrected it, but it cost me some time to do that. By the time we reached the DMV, it was too late to take the test.

THE GROWTH PROCESS WORKS, AND FINDING TRUE CONNECTION IS WORTH IT.

My son was very discouraged and sad. He had planned and prepared so long for this. His friends had been texting him on his cell phone to cheer him on. And now there was nothing, and it would be awhile before there was another opportunity to take the test. I felt very bad for him. In his teenage perspective, it was a really big deal. I told him, "I am really sorry about this. This was my fault, and you must be really bummed out and disappointed. This is a big deal." He nodded his agreement.

It was a long drive home. As teens do, my son had withdrawn and become silent in the car. He was not as much mad at me as he was simply disappointed and sad. Within a few minutes, feelings of guilt and words of self-condemnation began appearing inside my mind: *You really hurt your son. He was really looking forward to this, and what should have been a great experience for him will be a disappointing memory. Way to go, Dad.* This was a painful time, and I felt worse and worse.

Then, gradually, without my really consciously doing or thinking anything, new and different experiences and thoughts began to emerge inside. It wasn't intentional; it simply happened. I started to think, *Is there any solution that will help things here?* I began to problem-solve instead of beating myself up. I said, "I'm going to shift some stuff around tomorrow morning and get you out of your first-period class. Let's get this done." My son agreed to the new plan. It did not instantly change his feelings, as emotions don't always move that quickly. I also still felt bad for him and really wanted things to be instantly better for him. That didn't happen. But what did change was what I was doing inside with the situation. I was more concerned about him than in beating myself up, which is useless. I was working on finding a good solution. I was feeling remorseful but not guilty. And I was reconciled to where things were at that point in time. In other words, the connected state took over at some point during that drive. Your sense of being bonded and attached will also help you in your own times of failure, stress, and difficulty.

The task of connectedness involves making sure you are attached. And it always involves needing, asking, receiving, and using love and care. Learn these, experience these, and benefit from these. These keys to connectedness are not simply your foundation for learning how to relate to others; they are your foundation for life itself.

GOD AND BEING CONNECTED

Ultimately, becoming and remaining a connected person is about spirituality and about God himself. Connecting is a process of which God is the Author, Creator, and Sustainer. He is intimately involved in all the intricacies of your being attached. This is so much a part of who God is, it is vital that you understand his role in your being connected both to him and to others. Then you can cooperate with him in your own role. Here are some of the ways he operates with connectedness.

First, God's nature is that of a connected and attached being. The mysterious reality of the Trinity—Father, Son, and Spirit—illustrates this. In a fashion that we cannot fully comprehend, God is always attached, giving and receiving within this reality. No matter how disconnected humanity becomes from him, he is never isolated from relationship. And his permanent connectedness enables him to continue providing the resources of life for us: "May the grace of the Lord

THESE KEYS TO CONNECTEDNESS ARE NOT SIMPLY YOUR FOUNDATION FOR LEARNING HOW TO RELATE TO OTHERS; THEY ARE YOUR FOUNDATION FOR LIFE ITSELF.

Jesus Christ, and the love of God, and the fellowship of the Holy Spirit be with you all."[11]

God also created the process we are dealing with in this chapter, that the connectors must be connected. He created the universe to be a place where receiving and giving are good and necessary things, where connectedness is how things are and how things happen. For example, in the world of physics and mathematics, the chaos theory says that seemingly random events and systems are actually related in some underlying order. The suspense movie *The Butterfly Effect* is based on this theory. There is a connection, even when it is not seen. In the same way, God designed us to be connected and to need each other, to be in relationship. From the beginning of Creation, God made it clear that it is not good for us to be alone.[12] That verse in the Bible is often understood to refer to marriage; however, it encompasses all human relationships. We need God, and we need people, and we are not fully complete until we have both in our lives.

This is important, because disconnected people often spiritualize their hurt and empty condition and try to see a bad thing as a good thing. Not wanting to make God the problem, or simply not understanding how the Bible teaches that needing people is good, they will take the attitude that all they need is God and his love and attempt to do away with their need for people. This sounds spiritual, but it simply is not a biblical teaching. Here are a few examples among many of how clearly the Bible shows that we are to need people who are "God with skin on":

- King Solomon's observation: "If one person falls, the other can reach out and help. But someone who falls alone is in real trouble."[13]

- Jesus' words to the disciples during his time of need: "Then He said to them, 'My soul is deeply grieved, to the point of death; remain here and keep watch with Me.'"[14]

- The apostle Paul's experience of having someone connect in his discouragement: "But God, who encourages those who are discouraged, encouraged us by the arrival of Titus."[15]

- Peter's teaching that we bring God's grace to one another: "As each one has received a special gift, employ it in serving one another as good stewards of the manifold grace of God."[16]

The point is that God loves us every day, in more than one way, and he designed things so that we are to be connected to him directly, and by him indirectly, through people. That is normal and good. The person who experiences only a need for God and no need to open up to people is not someone who is relating the way the Scriptures teach us to. He is incomplete.

So if you can identify with the disconnected state, whether it be mild, moderate, or severe, bring it to God and ask for his help. Let him know that you want to make the connection to him, to trust and belong to him. Ask God to help you experience his love—from his Word, his Spirit, and his people. He will answer that prayer because it is what he wants for all of us.

I have seen this happen in many people, personally and professionally. It has had a permanent effect on me at many levels. I have been in small groups for many years, for example, and have experienced the grace, acceptance, empathy, validation, and understanding of God, both directly and indirectly, in these meetings. I cannot imagine where I would be today without the hours and hours spent with these people. There is no substitute. More than that, there is no more spiritual answer than this.

CONNECTION BEFORE CHANGE

Not long ago, I was working with some people on creating a resource for small groups. We were devising ways to help people have better quality and more intimate small-group experiences so that they could be safe and grow spiritually and emotionally. One aspect of the resource was training small groups on how to help a group member who was going through a crisis, anything from a major health issue to a divorce. People often don't know what to do or say in this sort of a situation, and small groups can be very powerful in helping individuals walk through a devastating time of life.

I was talking to Margaret, a team member on the project who is an effective connector, about what small groups can say to a person in a crisis, especially when that person is thinking about leaving the group. Sometimes a person in a difficult time of life will think that their issue is too heavy or serious for a group, or that he will be too much of a drain, so he will want to quit. Margaret and I came up with several things small group members could say to that person. For example, "We want especially to help you during this time of life, not just the good times." Or "We don't feel you are a drain; we want to be there for you." These are helpful ideas. But Margaret came up with the best reason of all: "We would miss you if you left." That statement added a very important piece to what love and relationships are all about, which is that *connecting must be from the heart, not just because it is good for us.*

Margaret's comment shows an important point about connection. Connecting ultimately serves and assists personal growth and change, as does anything valuable or significant in life. It builds a bridge and makes it safe to do the work of transformation that we all need. But at the same time, *you must connect whether or not the other person changes.* That person needs to know that, first and foremost, you are concerned about him as a person *as he is right now, today.* You accept and care about him irrespective of his actions. You certainly hope that he begins to grow and that your care moves him along that path. But you will not abandon him if he doesn't make the moves you want.

ASK GOD TO HELP YOU EXPERIENCE HIS LOVE— FROM HIS WORD, HIS SPIRIT, AND HIS PEOPLE. HE WILL ANSWER THAT PRAYER BECAUSE IT IS WHAT HE WANTS FOR ALL OF US.

People cannot and will not change if they think you do not accept them where they are. It simply will not happen, at least on a permanent level. They need the unconditional, relational safety that you will connect with them regardless. Otherwise, they will resist your attempts at connection and not let you in. Why should they? Would you open up to someone who said, in effect, "Do the work of letting me get to know you, but remember that if you don't become the new person I'd like, all that goes away"? Most of us would never take on that project. It would be too risky, too painful. We would probably prefer finding some other nongrowing and nonchanging person who has no interest in transformation . . . but who connects with us anyway.

You must remember that connection comes before change in your loving relationships. For example, I had a client, Marie, who came in with depression and a struggling marriage. As I worked with her in the initial stages, I could see the issues driving both problems. They seemed pretty straightforward and made sense, and in fact, I believe these issues were real. Since the issues and their resolution seemed clear to me, I began to make clarifications and some suggestions about what would help. Some of her issues were about problems in her family of origin, some were about the way she conducted her life and relationships, and some were about things I thought she needed to face and let go of.

I expected Marie to give me the usual resistance that most clients give, which is normal. Change isn't easy, and part of therapy is facing fears and feelings that are uncomfortable. So resistance is part of the process. People often disagree, object, divert, and withdraw to stay safe from the transformational work. But ultimately, once things are safe enough, and they are ready, they make the changes and move on.

Yet Marie's resistance was greater than almost any client I had ever seen. She did not just disagree; she exploded. She did not just object; she vehemently argued. She did not just divert; she created crises that got us off track. She did not just withdraw; she almost terminated therapy. It was a very challenging time for both of us. I could not figure why Marie was so opposed to the growth process. I got extra supervision for a colleague to understand what was happening.

> CONNECTING MUST BE FROM THE HEART, NOT JUST BECAUSE IT IS GOOD FOR US.

Finally, in one session I began to get it. I asked Marie, "Is it possible that you feel like I am pushing you too hard?" Marie's face changed and almost instantly looked more open. She said, "Yes! You are too pushy! You want me to change and face things and take responsibility and all that. But you are going too fast. Slow down! You haven't heard me yet."

"Haven't heard what?" I asked.

"The rest of me," she said. "I have more to tell you about what kind of person I am and what I have done. There are some things you need to know. I don't know if you're still going to be there for me when you hear these parts. But I know I will not ever change until you know me."

Fortunately, I listened to what Marie was saying. I slowed down the pace. I held off on my perspectives, clarifications, and suggestions. And I connected, working hard to understand what I had been not hearing and for Marie to know she was being understood. She continued to talk about her life, her feelings, her fears, her past, her spiritual experiences, her mistakes. She opened up about matters she had not brought up before. And I continued to listen and connect.

Somehow, down the line the relationship had passed some sort of a test for Marie—the test of safety. I knew that because she said during one session, "OK, I think I'm ready for your feedback." She had told me enough about herself, and the connection had been maintained, so she was safe. I began to point out things, to interpret what they meant, to confront issues, and to make suggestions. And Marie, still with some hesitation but with a great deal of courage, received my words and began to make the changes she needed to make. In time, her depression resolved and her marriage was greatly improved.

It is important to note here that Marie was not avoiding growth. She wasn't trying to distract herself from what she had to face and own. In fact, Marie was not even preparing for growth, or getting herself ready for the process. *She was actually growing during this time.* She was confessing who she was, risking the relationship, and facing her fears of loss of acceptance and connection. It was just a different part of the transformation process.

Had I continued the way I had been going, I am convinced that Marie would have eventually quit counseling and not returned, perhaps to any therapist. She would have remained convinced that people didn't want to connect to her for her sake, only for the results.

You, as a loving person, need to remember this. If other people think that you only care about who they will become in the future, they will quickly and consistently resist your attempts to connect. They do not want you to look at them as you would a remodeling project, focusing on what things will look like after you "fix it." People want the relationship to be, as the old hymn says, "just as I am."

THE ROLE OF PAIN

Having said that, this doesn't mean that if you have suffered in relationships, or have been deprived of them, that you are not a connecting person or that you cannot become one. Some people feel disqualified from being a loving person because of a difficult childhood, marriage, or relationship. They wonder if they are damaged goods and are relegated to being a spectator in connections, but not a provider.

This is not true at all. Some of the warmest and most caring connectors are people who have been deeply hurt and wounded. They have suffered all sorts of relational injury, such as withdrawal of love, criticism, and being controlled, abused and traumatized. And they are able to provide warmth and grace to those in their lives in very meaningful ways. How is this possible? If it is true that the more we receive the more we can give, shouldn't the converse also be true? Since I have received the bad, do I have little good to give?

There are a couple of reasons that hurt people can be connectors. One has to do with our values, what is important to us. Our values form our choices, direction, and paths in life. You may not have received a lot of the right kinds of love. And that may not have been your

IF OTHER PEOPLE THINK THAT YOU ONLY CARE ABOUT WHO THEY WILL BECOME IN THE FUTURE, THEY WILL QUICKLY AND CONSISTENTLY RESIST YOUR ATTEMPTS TO CONNECT.

choice; in fact, most of the time it is not our choice. But even though you have suffered from relational hurt, you can still have a value for connection and for relationship. That is, anyone can say, "I can't reach out, but I know it is a good thing, and I want to do this." That is a value. And values drive and motivate us to enter the process of healing and caring.

The other reason is that the presence of relationships that hurt you does not end things. That is not your final state. It means you need to take the efforts to get the right kinds of relationships from the right kinds of people. The good can heal what happened with the bad, and that is a vital reality that you need to experience and take risks on.

Sometimes this happens to us inadvertently, without a lot of direction on our own. It is more an example of God stepping in and protecting us when we can't protect ourselves. For example, Nicole, whom you met earlier in this chapter, did not come from a loving, warm family. There were lots of problems, including a very detached and self-absorbed mother. Nicole's mom had very little to offer her, and Nicole was injured by this. However, her grandmother was a warm, accessible, and present person. She spent a great deal of time with Nicole, just listening, talking, and providing the warmth Nicole needed. Grandma had the resources for Nicole, and she loved deeply. This relationship continued during Nicole's developmentally formative years and probably saved her from some serious emotional problems as a little girl. In fact, when her grandmother passed away, it was a bigger loss for Nicole than when her mom died. Her story is a perfect illustration of how "God places the lonely in families"[17] when their original families do not have what is needed.

> EVEN THOUGH YOU HAVE SUFFERED FROM RELATIONAL HURT, YOU CAN STILL HAVE A VALUE FOR CONNECTION AND FOR RELATIONSHIP.

Then, as we grow up, we need to choose the right relationships. This doesn't mean that God has stopped protecting. It means we are to take some of the responsibility, because we are more able than we were as kids. We are to find and attach ourselves to emotionally healthy people who can help us finish the job of being a loved person. That is where nurturing churches, small groups, mentors, guides, coaches, therapists, and all sorts of helping people become important. These connections can happen in your early years, and they can happen in your later years. The point is, connection needs to happen, and that set of experiences can heal the bad ones and provide you with what you need to be a connector.

The pain you experienced then becomes a teacher for you. You can draw upon memories and the lessons learned and become deeply compassionate, patient, and graceful with others. Your hurt makes you more aware of, and sensitive to, the hurts of others. We will deal more extensively with this in the chapter on healing.

Pain in and of itself is not a great thing, and I never like it when someone is told, "What you are going through will be good for you." That is simply not always true if no one is around to connect and help. Yet pain plus love and comfort can result in transformation, and that is the design for all of us.

I recently had a theological discussion with a friend about pain and love. He didn't see why people can't simply move on from hurtful relationships and experiences. "Sometimes people just need to stop complaining and get on with life," he said.

I replied, "Sure, there are chronic complainers. But I have seen you with your kids. When they were little, what did you do when they tripped and banged their knees on the floor? Did you say, 'Stop complaining and get on with life'?"

"No," he acknowledged. "I picked them up and held them till they were OK."

I continued. "You are right, we are to move on from pain. But often we can't move on until there is comfort in the picture. That gives us the wherewithal to put it behind us."

My friend got it, and I hope you get it too. When you have been unloved and hurt, get the comfort you need. Then you will be able to become a connector.

THE ABILITIES OF A CONNECTING PERSON

Let's return to my friend Nicole for a minute. You might be tempted to think that she is one of those lucky people who has a special ability to connect and that you could never do what she does. You think Nicole's story is not a realistic example of how you could be as a loving person.

While no one could deny that Nicole is naturally gifted in connecting, that doesn't mean we can't learn from her, be inspired by her, and become a very effective and competent connector. I know Nicole well enough to know that she is intentional about being with and understanding others, and what that involves. The best models for anything, from relationships to business to sports, are those with the gift who also worked hard at it at the same time. The "Nicole factor" involves some effort and hard work; it's no miracle.

People often discount the work, growth, and skills involved in connecting. They will say, "Well, connection just comes out of people like Nicole. It's just a

> WHEN YOU HAVE
> BEEN UNLOVED AND
> HURT, GET THE
> COMFORT YOU NEED.
> THEN YOU WILL
> BE ABLE TO BECOME
> A CONNECTOR.

part of them. It's so natural that they don't even think about it." This sort of thinking is just not true, and is usually a defense against hoping, or trying, or working on changing. My point is you were designed to connect by God, just as you were designed to be a loved person—and just as the entire universe is built around love and connecting. Don't deny the way life is structured because it hasn't worked for you in the past.

God and growth are all about new starts and new beginnings. I have seen many, many people learn to connect with others on deep, intimate, and helpful levels. There is no reason for you to think that you are disqualified from this ability, and there are many reasons to be hopeful about making progress and having success.

TAKE THE INITIATIVE

Connections do not simply happen between two people. They exist because someone took the first step. People who want to connect seek out the person they care about and take the initiative to make contact. They do not wait for things to fall into place or for the other person to make the first move. Not only that, but you are to take the initiative in moving the conversation and the relationship deeper, as we will explain in the next section.

Taking the initiative in any relationship, whether it be a new or an established one, involves some effort and some risk. It is work to get out of our routines and seek out someone by making a phone call or an appointment. It is much easier to wait until the other person asks or has a need. This is what is called a passive stance rather than an active one.

A passive stance can cause relational problems for you. For one thing, healthy and mature people get tired of making all the effort, so they will tend to invest more in relationships in which initiative is shared more. You risk losing the healthy people in your life, or at least as much involvement as you might like with them, by remaining passive in the relationship. For another thing, with a passive stance you are not truly taking ownership of your desire to connect. You are shuffling that off to someone else, and you will not develop this ability to the degree that you will experience its benefits. I have a friend who is taking dance lessons on a weekly basis. She is getting pretty good at it. And she is constantly looking for people to practice with, go to dance clubs with, and talk to about dance. And that is why she keeps improving.

Connection is not a passive process. There is certainly risk involved. Making the call or asking for more of a relationship than there already is offers the other person the freedom to say, "No, I am not interested in getting together, or having coffee, or in getting to know each other better; I'm fine." For some people, that prospect is enough to shut them down from taking the first step. Often, they have had hurtful relationship experiences in the past, and they don't want to repeat them. No one could blame them for wanting to avoid that. However, the real solution is to heal, get better, let

> GOD AND GROWTH ARE ALL ABOUT NEW STARTS AND NEW BEGINNINGS.

go, grieve, or whatever you need to do so that you can begin taking risks again. It is never a good idea to make a permanent commitment to avoiding risk because you might get hurt. You run a greater risk of avoiding a good life than you do of getting hurt again.

Learn to say, "Can we talk? Want to have lunch together? I would like to spend some time with you. Are you free anytime in the next week or so? Can I talk to you about how things are going?" There are many ways to take the initiative. You may not do it well at first, but so what? Practice makes perfect. We would all do well to take an active position in connecting with others.

MOVE FROM THE EVERYDAY TO THE EMOTIONAL

The ability to connect requires you to move deeper with another person. Most connections begin with the everyday and move to the emotions. That is just how process tends to happen, unless it is a more focused setting, such as counseling or a relationally based small group. These heart issues may concern those everyday events, and they may not. But the important thing is to be able to gradually help the person experience his or her feelings and for you to be there with those feelings.

Most of the time, this emotional connection can be accomplished by your own response to what the person is saying or talking about. That is, you connect by providing deeper or more emotional responses to what is being said. That, in turn, helps the other person become safer, more vulnerable, and more heart-based. The process is a little like what happens when you have a computer problem and are on the phone with a skilled technical support person. He instructs you to go into certain files and programs in order to help find the source of the problem. Down you go, into, for example, the registry, where if you are not careful, a wrong move can damage your computer. But the tech helps you open files and folders each step of the way. In the same way, you, as the connector, provide levels of empathy and understanding that help the person experience himself at more real levels.

> TAKING THE INITIATIVE IN ANY RELATIONSHIP, WHETHER IT BE A NEW OR AN ESTABLISHED ONE, INVOLVES SOME EFFORT AND SOME RISK.

For example, suppose you are a married man talking to your wife at night after the kids are asleep. Here is a sample conversation that demonstrates moving deeper:

He: "So how was your day?"

She: "I am beat. We had quarterly reports due at work, and then when the school called about picking up Genny because of her cold, that made things worse."

He: "That's a lot to handle at one time."

She: "It's a lot. And I had to rush the report because I was leaving for school."

He: "Do you think it didn't go well?"

She: "I'm not sure, but I wonder."

He: "That would be a little scary, knowing about the downsizing and everything going on there."

She: "Yes, I am scared. If I didn't do a good job, it could be bad for me."

He: "Sorry it's so scary, honey. How bad is it?"

She: "I haven't said a lot to you because I know you have your stress too. But I'm starting to become afraid. What will happen to us if I get demoted or fired?"

He: "If we don't have your income, we will deal with it. But are you feeling something else too?"

She: "I think I am. I think I'm more afraid of how not having my income will affect us, our marriage, the kids, and our relationship with each other. I don't want anything to hurt who we are."

He: "It would affect our lifestyle, sure. But you and I are a lot more than lifestyle. We're a team. I'm on your side. If something bad happens in your job, we'll deal with it like we always do. I never want you to walk around scared all day. We're together, and jobs aren't going to affect how I feel about you."

She: (visibly moved) "Thanks. I was more anxious than I realized. It's nice to have you listen to me."

He: "Sure."

Notice in this interchange how much ground the couple covered in just a few minutes: all the way from the wife's everyday fatigue to her deeper fears of the relationship suffering. Her husband was able to help things get to a level where she really experienced what she was afraid of so he could then reassure and comfort. This in turn brought a new and better level of connection. What was required were empathetic statements, focusing on her experience, and asking open-ended questions. Most people readily respond to these and are waiting for you to help them connect on a meaningful level.

This is not to say that knowing about someone, as opposed to knowing someone's heart, as happened above, is not valuable. Everyday conversations are helpful and very important in connecting and being a loving person. Connection does involve these other aspects of what people do when they get together. People talk about their families, jobs, and activities. They connect about their opinions, values, and observations. They tell jokes and talk about politics, sports, and weather. These are all important and normal parts of human interaction. Often, these aspects are a way to introduce people to each other, and in that way, they are a preparation for true connection.

This chapter has shown how the process of moving deeper is something any-one can learn and do. However, in the best relationships, connecting is something both people do with each other. That is, good relationships are a two-way street; each individual has an active interest in learning more about the heart of the other and helping that person experience more of himself. But even if the other person is not connecting, go ahead and connect. Make that the norm in the relationship, and gradually require it of the other person. It is good for both of you.

SUSPEND YOUR POINT OF VIEW

I was sitting on a plane, writing this chapter, when the movie *The Pursuit of Happyness,* featuring Will Smith, came on. I hadn't seen it and wanted to keep writ-ing, so I tuned it out. But about an hour into the presentation, I looked over at the woman next to me, who was watching. She had tears rolling down her cheeks, and an observant flight attendant even came by and gave her a tissue. I figured this was a movie I should see, so I asked her when it was over, "Is it pretty good?"

"It's sort of depressing," she said. "He goes through some awful things. But he comes out OK, and it's a good ending." This woman was doing what we all do when we see well-crafted movies. She had identified with the main character and temporarily lost herself in his life, struggle, emotions, and inspi-ration. That is why we love movies: we get out of ourselves and experience someone else's life in a way that then builds us up inside.

This is a lot like an aspect of what connecting people do. They are temporarily able to put aside their own experiences and perspective and enter the world of the other person. Loving people who connect place their spin on things on the back burner while they are connecting. This helps them see what it is like to be in some-one else's shoes, and it is a powerful and effective part of connecting.

Think about the last time you spent time with a connecting person, maybe in the same way Amanda was with Nicole. Most likely you came away from that encounter feeling something like this: *She understands me. I don't have to explain or defend myself. I can just talk and she seems to know what I am really saying and feeling.* You have been with someone with empathy.

As I mentioned in an earlier chapter, empathy is the ability to share some-one's feelings. All of us need empathy. And when we receive it, it enables us to give it. Why is this so important? Because empathy *helps us not feel alone.* When you empathize with another person, you are "in there" with them: their memories, their viewpoint, their emotions, and their values.

For those few minutes that you lose yourself in the other person, he is able to tolerate, look at, and deal with who he is, for he is connected in relationship, not all by himself, with himself.

IN THE BEST RELATIONSHIPS, CONNECTING IS SOMETHING BOTH PEOPLE DO WITH EACH OTHER.

Empathy is actually spiritual in nature and design. God is the most empathic being in the universe. He feels what we feel, and he readily enters our world. In fact, the reality of the person of Jesus is the highest act of empathy ever. God became human, experiencing all the emotions, struggles, limitations, and joys of being a person. In so doing, he showed us that he does know what it is like to be us, which serves to comfort us, encourage us, and help us listen to his words, for he has earned the right for us to hear him: "Since he himself has gone through suffering and testing, he is able to help us when we are being tested."[18] The model of connecting empathically comes from God—through him and his people to us.

Empathy is not natural, but it is spiritual instead.

Being an empathic connector is work. It is not always easy for us to set aside how we see things. In fact, *empathy is not natural, it is spiritual.* It is natural to consider your own feelings instead of the other's; it is spiritual to cast those aside for the time being. It is natural to insist that the other person should understand your point of view first. It is spiritual to be patient and hear them out. It is natural to correct their distorted viewpoint. It is spiritual to find out what their experience is. That is work, but I do not know of a task that brings more and better fruit in relationships than this. It is worth it to give up what comes naturally for what is spiritual, resulting in the best outcome.

ELEMENTS OF THE CONNECTION TIME

How do you suspend your point of view and empathize with others? Here are some of the elements that help you develop this skill.

DECIDE THAT FOR NOW, IT'S NOT ABOUT YOU; IT'S ABOUT THEM

Loving people are secure enough that they do not need everyone to understand and agree with them. The internalized love is enough to draw on. So they can afford to give up the demand to be heard, validated, and empathized with for this period. That is what grown-ups do. For now, the other person is more important than their need to be understood.

EMPATHY IS NOT NATURAL, IT IS SPIRITUAL.

Some people never make this connection, and they have tremendous difficulty in relationships. They consistently require that everyone see things their way, and it becomes costly. Unhealthy people will allow it and then cause conflict. Healthy people will either confront it or leave the relationship.

While suspending your point of view in favor of another's takes some work, once you get into the habit of "it's not about me right now," you will find the discipline enjoyable. What are you learning about this person? You become broader, become richer, and have a greater capacity to love and connect. The loving person always gets something back by leaving his experience for another's welfare.

FOCUS, FOCUS, FOCUS

As we have seen again and again in this chapter, connection is work. It requires you to shut out distractions and other concerns in your mind. It does not simply happen in some mystical, effortless way. We must be intentional about concentrating on listening to the other person's underlying themes, emotions, and heart issues. When you think about the fact that it's time for an oil change, you either set that thought aside internally or, if you can't, say "excuse me" and write a one-word note on a piece of paper so that thought has a home to stay in.

Focus on the other person more than you focus on what he is thinking about you, or if you are doing a good job, or how long this will last. Remember that *our minds sometimes create distractions to get away from the connection.* We actually divert ourselves from concentrating on intimacy because it can be risky or fatiguing. So take ownership of the distractions from concentrating, and focus on the relationship with the other person.

WHILE THE PERSON IS TALKING, ASK YOURSELF, WHAT IS IT LIKE FOR HIM RIGHT NOW?

In other words, become curious about the other person's framework. Is he feeling afraid? Powerless? Frustrated? Bugged? Sad? Joyous? The more interested and curious you are about the other person's state of mind, the better able you will be to empathize with him.

Stay in the present moment with the other person. Don't get lost in the paralysis of analysis right at this point. Remember the last time you lost yourself in a movie, playing a sport, or doing a hobby you enjoy? The more you are in the moment with another, the less you will think about the passage of time, and that is good. You will become more involved and accessible to the person.

WHEN YOU IDENTIFY HOW THE PERSON IS FEELING, FEEL IT YOURSELF

The ability not only to know what the other person is feeling, but to allow yourself to feel their emotions as much as possible is a critical part of the connection process. This is often uncomfortable, because most of the time empathy has to do with painful feelings. But it does a huge work in building the bridge. Go ahead and let it happen.

For example, I was talking to James, a friend of mine. He told me a little of his own story. His dad abandoned him at an early age, leaving James's mom to fend for herself and the kids. They went through years of poverty and struggle. Years later, by a series of unusual circumstances, he encountered his dad as a teen.

By then, though he had had a very difficult adolescence, he had found Christ and was part of a healthy church with people who genuinely loved him and helped him get through. James told me that he felt a multitude of feelings, seeing his dad, but the dominant one was that, even though he felt angry and hurt, he also felt love and compassion for him, and he reached out and embraced his dad.

As he was telling me this part of his tale, tears came to my eyes. I found myself feeling a great deal of compassion for James's situation and what he had gone through. I experienced emotions of

LOVING PEOPLE ARE SECURE ENOUGH THAT THEY DON'T NEED EVERYONE TO UNDERSTAND AND AGREE WITH THEM.

aloneness, of being lost and abandoned, and finally of celebration for his final connection with his father. I was not feeling my friend's emotions. That is not possible; we don't actually feel each other's feelings. But I was feeling my own emotions as they identified with his experience.

ACTIONS, WORDS, AND EXPERIENCES

Connecting is more than simple action and behavior. It cannot be summarized on a concrete to-do list with the guarantee that you will have successfully connected. But at the same time, that doesn't mean that connecting is some mystical abstraction that you have to be in a "zone" to enter. This thinking tends to discourage people who have a hard time with feelings. The reality is that connecting involves the heart; therefore it is spiritual and emotional. It involves what we do, so it also involves action. Connecting also brings in our words, as that is how we convey what we feel and think. *Connecting requires doing, saying, and experiencing.* Connectors are involved with all three of these.

Let me give you an example. I recently had lunch with Tom, a business acquaintance. During our time together, he mentioned that he had received some medical test results that indicated he was having prostate problems. I didn't know Tom well, but I was concerned, as these issues can be serious. However, Tom had said it offhandedly, as if it was no big deal.

> THE ABILITY NOT ONLY TO KNOW WHAT THE OTHER PERSON IS FEELING BUT TO ALLOW YOURSELF TO FEEL THEIR EMOTIONS AS MUCH AS POSSIBLE IS A CRITICAL PART OF THE CONNECTION PROCESS.

I have found that it is common for people to do this. They bring up some subject they are scared or concerned about, but in a way that indicates they don't have any real feelings about it, such as, "So the doctor gave me some numbers about my prostate and said there might be a problem, but you never know about this. Anyway, how is business?" In my experience, these people are afraid to say what they really feel, but they do want a connection. So this casual manner is a way to approach the other person and see if there is a warm response.

I have also found that *when a person mentions a problem, you can hardly ever go wrong by following up on that problem.* That is an essential part of connection. Most of the time, a person really desires the contact but just doesn't have the knowledge, awareness, or courage to talk about it with the gravity that they are feeling it.

Here is what I did with Tom to help connect him, and you will see that there are both experiences and actions involved in the contact.

I felt how scared I would be if I had gotten bad news from my doctor. I experienced my own fear, anxiety, and confusion over not knowing how severe things were.

I experienced compassion for Tom and his anxiety. I felt an empathic and warm feeling for him, and how tough it must be for him right now.

I leaned forward to better focus on this moment with him. I didn't want to miss, or for Tom to miss, what he might be needing right now.

I looked at him in the eyes so that he would know I was available and accessible, and also so I would be able to really concentrate on Tom and how he was doing.

I said, "I'm sorry about the test results. How is that for you?" I wanted him to know that I wanted ed to talk about something unpleasant if he did. I spoke broadly ("How is that for you?" instead of "How are you feeling?") because I wanted him to have room to move away or toward the emotions as he saw fit.

I restrained myself from laughing nervously along with him when Tom said, "Well, guess it's time to find another doctor." I did not want to go along with Tom's defensiveness just yet, as lots of people will do that and then settle into the real thing. If he had continued, I would have probably gone along and changed the subject with him, as we weren't close, but at that point I did want him to have an opportunity to go there.

CONNECTING REQUIRES DOING, SAYING, AND EXPERIENCING. CONNECTORS ARE INVOLVED WITH ALL THREE OF THESE.

I said, "That has to be scary" and "Tell me more" when he began to open up about his fears of being sick or even dying. I wanted Tom to know he wasn't alone with those feelings, and they had a place in our relationship. And I didn't want a lot of my own views present, as he needed room for his own experience and a lot of safety at that time.

Within a few minutes, Tom was able to talk about his fears and concerns. He seemed relieved, and even said, "Wow, I didn't even know I had these feelings. It was good to get this off my chest; I feel better now." So a combination of actions, words, and experiences, along with Tom's hard work and willingness, were part of the connection equation.

Most people who want to grow in loving and connecting find that they are less sure of themselves with the experiencing and words aspects than the action parts. They believe that they can handle a set of specific instructions such as "have eye contact," "use empathetic responses," and "lean forward" a lot more competently than they can handle being told to "feel and experience." It seems vague and difficult for them to get their arms around it.

However, the best answer to this problem is simple: *provide what you have received.* That is, remember that in order to connect, you must be in the process of being a loved person. And for that to be a reality, someone out there sat down with you and gave actions, words, and experiences that conveyed to you that you were safe, valuable, and understood. So if you are loved, it is in you already. Turn it around and give back what you have gained.

When I encounter this with a person in the counseling office, it is, more often than not, actually a sign that the individual is having difficulty in receiving love and care. When I hear their concern, I take it as a signal to explore with them the possibility that they do not live in the loved state, or are having some problem taking care in. Then, if that is what is going on, we work on them getting the connection for themselves. And it is likely that, as that resolves, their capacity to connect on an experience level is much easier. You cannot make yourself feel compassion for someone you care about. But you can draw on your own experiences, memories and feelings of what that has been like for you. It will help you to help them.

REMEMBER THAT IN ORDER TO CONNECT, YOU MUST BE IN THE PROCESS OF BEING A LOVED PERSON.

FOLLOW THE LEADER

One of the most important and difficult parts of learning to connect is that you will need to give up control of how you are received and experienced by the other person. That person, and only that person, will determine whether you have successfully connected with them, especially in the aspect of hearing what they are saying. You can listen, use positive body language, try to feel feelings, and use empathic words all day and all night. You can let them know how much you care, and how much you want them to feel connected. But there is one thing you cannot do: you can't demand that the person respond, open up, appreciate your time, and feel connected. That is up to the other person, not you.

The reality is that connection is a two-way street. You cannot do all the work, though you must do a lot. The other person must do work as well. There is effort involved in receiving; it is not a passive experience. You, the connector, can take a great deal of responsibility to do your job in connecting. But you cannot take all of the responsibility. It must be shared with the "connectee." So it stands to reason that you cannot be in total control of whether or not the person feels connected with you. That person must guide you and respond to you in ways that help you know if connection is working. You must be humble, be flexible, and listen to see if you are really listening.

For example, recently I was talking to a friend, Ray, who was concerned about his daughter and her marriage. She did not seem happy, and there were signs that Ray's son-in-law was part of the problem. Ray mentioned that the son-in-law was somewhat impulsive, especially with finances. He spent too much money on his hobbies and his friends, and he didn't save for his family. Also, Ray said that the young man seemed to be emotionally immature.

> THE REALITY IS THAT CONNECTION IS A TWO-WAY STREET. YOU CANNOT DO ALL THE WORK, THOUGH YOU MUST DO A LOT. THE OTHER PERSON MUST DO WORK AS WELL.

I grew angry inside at the son-in-law, whom I didn't know, which is often a mistake. I think because of that, I took a leap in my attempt to connect with Ray that I wouldn't normally take. I said, "Sounds like it's hard to like this guy, especially with how he affects your daughter."

Ray said, "No, that's not it. I do like him. He's involved with my daughter and the kids. He spends a lot of time with them, and I think he loves them. And I like being with him; he's basically a good-hearted guy. I just don't like how immature he is."

I said, "OK, it's not hard to like him. It's scarier to think that he may hurt his family's financial security in some way."

"Yes," said Ray. "That's what I'm really afraid of."

The conversation went on from there and ended well. But Ray's correction was helpful in focusing things in the direction he needed to go, which was his anxiety about his daughter's financial stability. I had to respond and listen to that, and follow his lead. If I had instead said, "No, I think you don't like him, and I agree with you that you shouldn't either. He is a bad influence on your daughter," I would have been trying to tell Ray how to feel. That never goes anywhere in connection. And that is why I say that connection requires you to be a humble person. Sometimes you have to make correction after correction after correction to finally get what someone feels or is saying. And that is a good thing, and worth the time and effort: "The purposes of a man's heart are deep waters, but a man of understanding draws them out."[19]

Everyone plays follow the leader in other areas of life. The last time you had a cold and cough and went to the doctor, if he was a good one, he asked you a series of questions. Each question was based on your answer to the previous one, and he continued until he told you whether you had a virus or an infection. He was serving your experience, following your answers. In fact, a doctor who would tell you what was wrong without thoroughly listening to your symptoms could be harmful. Or, if you are a parent, think about when your child was an infant and was crying. Babies cannot tell you what is wrong. So you had to work with her to figure that out, playing follow the leader. Is she hungry? Does she need changing? Is she lonely? Is she colicky? As you figure out what is making her cry, you are truly loving, because you are giving her some of the power to let you know if you understand or not.

As you follow the leader, you may be tempted to become frustrated with the other person. It might seem as though they do not appreciate how much work it is to connect, and the fine-tuning and correction may go unnoticed.

However, this is most likely about your own expectations of how things should go. Let go of the expectation and remember that it is not about you right now; it is about someone you want to connect with and love. This is simply part of the process. Most people are just giving you feedback by their words or actions as to whether you are hitting the mark.

One thing that helps in following the leader is to, at intervals, ask if you are getting it. This is simply checking in with the person. Get their responses and reactions about what is going on. This simple technique can save you hours of going down the wrong road. Say things like, "Is that what you're saying?" "Do I get it?" "Is that anywhere close to what is going on for you?" "Are we talking about what you are really feeling?" People genuinely appreciate and respond to that sort of openness. You and the other person are a team. You have what they need, but you need them to help you give it.

A PROCESS MORE THAN AN EVENT

People who are able to love well by connecting well do not look at the conversation as simply a one-time event. Though the illustrations and examples here are about a particular conversation or encounter with someone, that is not the total picture. Truly connecting at levels that convey love and care take more than one sitting or conversation, even though one event can help. What really changes lives is having repeated, structured, and committed times of connection with a person. I am talking here about a process of relationship, not an event.

It takes time for someone to trust you, to open up, to see that you are authentic, and to believe that you have something to offer. And that is just the beginning. After trust is established, it then takes time for the connection to address all different areas of a person's life. People need connection in many ways: about their marriages, dating relationships, friendships, families, kids, work issues, habits, and spiritual lives, to name a few. If you want your connections to count, do not be a "serial connector." Get in there for the long run, commit to the relationship, and get involved in the process. Do not believe what TV says about one dramatic lunch between two people changing a life. More often than not, that dramatic lunch had a lot of meetings and conversations prior to it that seeded and planted the process so that it would bear fruit at that lunch. Be patient. Make connection a way of life for your relationships. Few things offer better benefits over time.

HOW LONG IS ENOUGH?

All connecting conversations come to an end at some point. I have had meaningful connections that were a few seconds long and some that went for several hours. But there is a beginning, a middle, and an end to every connecting talk. You need to know when connection has been established, and when enough is enough. This is important, for you do not want to terminate the talk without the connection taking place. Nor do you want to continue indefinitely, when other life responsibilities must go on. Not only that, but ongoing conversations may be bad for the other person. Sometimes the attitude of "I am available at any time, for as long as you want" can create a lack of structure in the other person. It can keep the person from taking responsibility for using his or her time well with you, for time is finite and valuable, and it must be governed. Clear beginnings and endings are healthy for connection.

THE CONTEXT
Much of the time, circumstances will help determine how long the conversation must last. When people get together for coffee, lunch, or a meeting, there is usually an agreed-upon ending time. You both know that you will be paying the bill and leaving in an hour, so you keep that in mind. This should have some flexibility to it. It is difficult to talk about heart matters when someone is watching the clock in order to be precise. Often, when I am traveling and having a conversation on a cell phone while knowing my flight will be called in a couple of minutes, I will just say, "I'll have to call you back, I can't concentrate on what we are doing right now." I don't like to deal with deeper matters while preoccupied with other things.

THE TIME APART
Every connecting interaction has spaces of time, sometimes hours and sometimes weeks, between the conversations. Life must go on, and people are involved in their activities and other relationships. Connection time is actually

a minority of the time in our lives if you percentage it out against time for work, errands, functional conversations, casual conversations, alone time, and so on.

However, the time you are not connecting is not lost or dead time. It can be very fruitful and helpful time for you and the connection, in more than one way. For one thing, the time is useful for you to think about that person. Bring the person to mind, intentionally. He is important to you. His growth and well-being are important to you. Pray for him and ask God to help you connect with him the next time you see him, in a way that brings him the good he needs. Remember the last contact you had, and what happened. What did you talk about? Did he expose a feeling, a thought, or an experience that you want to remember and revisit the next time? Think through your relationship with the individual. Is something going on in his life that you have been missing or need to ask about? A big-picture perspective is a benefit when we use time apart.

As we call to mind the experiences we have internalized with people we care about, it also changes us inside. In a phrase, the love grows. We love the person more. Our capacity to care about him grows.

In fact, our capacity to care about other people grows. Remembering and being mindful of the valuable, emotional, and intimate times you have had with these people keeps you in touch with the loving feelings and values you have for them. That is why people use activities such as journaling and reflection during the day. Emotional memories are powerful, meaningful, and useful to you not just for this relationship but for the rest of your life.

IF YOU WANT YOUR CONNECTIONS TO COUNT, DO NOT BE A "SERIAL CONNECTOR." GET IN THERE FOR THE LONG RUN, COMMIT TO THE RELATIONSHIP, AND GET INVOLVED IN THE PROCESS.

Then there is the benefit that occurs inside the person with whom you are connecting. Remember that connection is not simply an experience of openness and intimacy that exists for its own sake. God uses and multiplies people's efforts to love each other, and that means that your connecting conversation's impact and influence is going on while you are apart from each other. The other person thinks about what you two said, how he experienced the time, how he experienced your presence, and what he felt. He ties that in to other events in his life and other people. He chews on thoughts and opinions you both aired. This work goes on in his conscious thoughts, his dreams, and his in-between times too. Like a slow cooker that takes eight hours to change an assortment of meat and vegetables into a stew, he is assimilating and working with the connection and making use of it. This can be valuable time fo that person, and good preparation for your next conversation.

THE TIME YOU INVEST TODAY IN A CONNECTION CAN BRING LONG-TERM BENEFITS TO THE OTHER PERSON.

I recently had a phone conversation with an old friend I do not see regularly, but we get together or talk when we can. The last time we talked, he mentioned a problem he had been having with his father, with whom he was in a business relationship as well. I did not remember spending a lot of time on his problem, as we roamed around several subjects. But on this recent phone call he said, "Last time we talked, you told me I wasn't letting my dad just be my partner. I was still wanting him to be the affirming person he has never been, so I resent him and try to please him in the business. Do you remember saying that?"

"Most of it," I said, trying to be honest, because I did not remember all of that conversation.

My friend continued. "Well, I've been mulling it over and over in the last few weeks. I realized this is the truth. I have to let Dad go and realize he can't or won't be a warm person with me. But he is good in business with me."

"How is it going?" I asked.

"It's working," my friend said. "He and I are getting along better, and the work is going better. I am having to deal with some sad feelings, I think I may need to let go and say good-bye to the dad I wanted. But that is OK too."

Here is the point: Time, the process, our relationship, and my friend's mulling it over produced good things. The time you invest today in a connection can bring long-term benefits to the other person.

TAKING THE NEXT STEPS

In this chapter we unpacked what connection is all about: when the relationship involves heart-to-heart contact. Remember that you must experience and receive connection in order to give it to others. And we went over the basics of how to connect with another person in words, experiences, and behaviors.

Along with the principles you have learned in this chapter, here are some final practical tips that will help you increase attachment, connection, and intimacy with others in your life:

- *Demystify connection in your mind.* Don't let the fact that connection is an incredible and powerful gift discourage you from learning the steps to connect. As we have learned, connection happens one step at a time. Just start trying it out, and it will keep getting better.

- *Start with people who have the ability to connect.* Suspending your point of view and going for the heart take work and effort, especially at first. Make the process simpler by first practicing with people you feel safe with, people familiar with the experience of connection.

- *Connection first, feelings second.* Don't wait until you feel loving to connect. Feelings are important, but they can't control your relationships. It is more about engagement. Get involved and start talking and listening. Often, the connection itself can change the emotions. If there are intense hurts that might get in the way, first tell someone who will listen and understand so that those emotions have a place to be processed.

- *Restrain the urge to advise.* Restrain the natural impulse to make helpful suggestions until you really understand the other person, until they really know you understand, and until you have talked about suggestions.

- *Trust God as the Connector.* Whenever you connect you are engaged in a process God designed and approves of and does better than anyone. Ask him for empathy, care, timing, and sensitivity. He wants you and that person to bridge the gap, as he does with us.

Although connectedness is an essential key to loving people, remember that it still does not encompass all of what love is. There are many connected people who are not very loving. They may feel secure, safe, and empathized with, but they may also be self-involved or disengaged from the process of loving others. All of us need the intent and desire to seek and do what is best, and we need the skill of truth-telling, which we will discuss in the following chapter.

F O U R

Truth-Telling: Solving Problems

Recently I had a conversation with Toni, a friend of mine whose kids are around the same age as our teenagers. I ran into her and her son Trevor at the grocery store. We were catching up with each other, and the subject of how the kids were doing came up. Toni mentioned that Trevor had been invited to a party of wild high schoolers where there would be underage drinking, and Trevor had declined. I said, "Trevor, way to go. Good choice." Toni smiled and said, "This is my good kid, you know."

I did not say anything at the time, but I was concerned. I thought that calling Trevor "my good kid" in front of him could cause problems for him. Though I am sure Toni did not mean it that way, it could convey several unhealthy attitudes toward Trevor: that she was in need of a good child, that his siblings weren't good kids, that his compliance made him love her more, or that if he got into trouble, she might love him less. The teenage years are important years for kids, offhanded statements can stay with them for a long time. Not only that, but I had heard Toni say things like that in passing several times before, such as, "He's easy," "You're my low-maintenance child," and "I wish your brother and sister were more like you." So there was a pattern, and I was worried about its effect on Trevor.

Toni is an involved and loving parent who does a very good job with her kids. I am a better dad from being around her mothering. So I had a lot of respect for her. But I knew that this was something significant. I began to think about how to bring this issue up to her.

It was not all that simple to figure out. I was unsure how Toni would take my observation. Would she be hurt? Would she withdraw? Get angry at me? Become defensive? I really cared about Toni and her family. We have known each other since the kids were small. I valued our friendship and our relationship. Above anything else, I did not want to alienate her. At the same time, I knew that I wanted to solve a potential problem for Trevor. So I figured out what I basically wanted to say. I didn't know how to set things up, though. I thought about a phone call or maybe asking to meet for coffee, but I felt stuck in that part.

Within a week, I saw Toni at a school function, so I figured this might be a good time. During a break, I asked her if she had a moment. We walked to a corner of the room. Toni asked, "What's up?"

I said, "I want to talk to you about a parenting thing. I think you are a really good parent, and I hope that you feel like you and I can talk about our kids honestly."

Toni looked a little reserved at that point, as I would have in her position. She said, "Well sure, I do feel that."

I continued. "I've noticed something in your relationship with Trevor that may be a little thing, but if it were me, I would want someone to bring it to my attention, OK?"

She looked a little more settled, I think because I had said, in effect, it was not a huge thing. "OK," Toni said.

"Several times in the past few months when I have seen you, you have referred to Trevor as your 'good kid,' or 'the low-maintenance one.'"

Toni jumped on that one. "Oh, I am so glad you said that! I was just wondering if that was going to be a bad thing for him!"

"What do you mean?" I asked.

"Well, you know, if you call a kid your 'good kid,' then he'll push back because he wants to be his own person and all that."

Toni had nailed it on the head. I said, "Yes, that's it. I think it causes a conflict inside teenagers, and then they try to resolve it by acting out to be themselves."

She said, "I know I have been doing it. It makes total sense that this isn't the best thing to do."

I was relieved. "I agree with you. And are you and I OK?"

The answer was immediate. "Absolutely. I'm so glad you mentioned it." I believed her. She had always been an honest and vulnerable person in our interactions, and there was no reason to doubt her.

I said, "And do I have your promise that if you see me doing anything weird in my parenting, that you'll talk to me?"

The answer was yes.

I have seen Toni several times since that brief encounter. She has been warm and engaging, as she always is. My fears had no basis in reality. But the point is, this is a good illustration of another aspect of loving people that everyone needs to work on and improve in order to seek the best for another. This chapter will lay out how to be not just a connecting person but also a confronting person.

LOVE MUST BE HONEST

As we have discussed, connection is extremely powerful and effective in learning to love others. By nature, connection seeks the best for, thinks well of, and wants good things for the other. And as we saw in the previous chapter, connection is sometimes all you need. Some people just need to be heard in order to feel loved and encouraged, move on, solve a problem, or face an issue.

Most of the time, however, connection is not enough. It is a necessary element of loving, but more is required to truly love another in ways that influence him or her to be a better, changing, growing person. And a large part of that is because people need to hear reality and truth, and they must learn to take responsibility for what they hear. This is not meant to sound harsh or mean, for love does not rejoice in someone getting their feelings hurt. But it does mean that being able to be honest—directly, lovingly, and effectively—goes a long way in being a true friend to anyone in your life.

I was talking to a woman after a speaking event, and she was telling me about the changes she had seen in her journey. One of the things she mentioned struck me: "I never used to tell the truth to anyone. No one knew

PEOPLE NEED TO HEAR REALITY AND TRUTH, AND THEY MUST LEARN TO TAKE RESPONSIBILITY FOR WHAT THEY HEAR.

when I disagreed about anything, emotionally or personally. But when I started being more honest, I found out a lot about my friends. Some of them liked me better and said, 'You go, girl.' But I had one I was very close to, and she ended the friendship. It was hard for me." I asked her how that was for her. She said, "It really hurt, but even with losing my friend, I could never go back to how I lived life before. I am out of jail, and I am going to stay that way. Honesty is the way to go."

LOVE TELLS THE TRUTH AND USES THE TRUTH TO BENEFIT THE OTHER PERSON.

Honesty is indeed the way to go. In fact, it is part and parcel of love itself. It cannot be divided from love. Loving people should tell the truth, and truthful people should be loving. They work hand in hand. A psalm describing God's own internal character says that in him, "Unfailing love and truth have met together. Righteousness and peace have kissed!"[1]

God's truthfulness and righteousness, and his connectedness and peace, are allies that are inextricably related. Just as God never shirks from either side, so are we designed to be connecting and honest.

Love tells the truth and uses the truth to benefit the other person.

HOW TRUTH SUPPORTS LOVE'S PURPOSE

Let's return to our definition of *love* as "seeking the best for the other," and look at how being truthful supports that effort. Love tells the truth and uses the truth to benefit the other person. There are several ways this happens.

TRUTH BRINGS AWARENESS

Many times, people simply may not know about a problem they are having. It may affect only them. It may affect others. And it may affect your connection with them. But for some reason, they may have a blind spot about this. You see the problem clearly, yet they live around it and miss it. One of the most caring things anyone can do for their loved ones is to make them aware of a behavior or attitude that is not good for them, for love, or for their growth.

All of us have blind spots. We can certainly be self-scrutinizing, soul-searching people, and that is a good thing. But you cannot know everything about yourself. Toni, whose story introduced the chapter, is a good example of a person who wasn't yet fully aware of a problem, though she may have been on the verge of it. When you bring awareness to someone you care about, you are simply telling that person what you observe is going on. You assume she genuinely does not know about it. In other words, *you are presuming innocence, not guilt,* on the other person's part.

ONE OF THE MOST CARING THINGS ANYONE CAN DO FOR THEIR LOVED ONES IS TO MAKE THEM AWARE OF A BEHAVIOR OR ATTITUDE THAT IS NOT GOOD FOR THEM, FOR LOVE, OR FOR THEIR GROWTH.

Even if you find out that that the person is aware of the problem, you are still better off presuming innocence first. That is a better mistake to make than judging someone unfairly. The repairs you will need to make are far less when you presume innocence.

As a psychologist, I have been amazed at how serious a problem someone can have, often for many years, and not be aware of it. One reason for this is that no one in their life has said anything, either thinking that they do not want to hurt the person's feelings or that the person already knows and has chosen to continue the behavior.

Here are some broad areas in which you may tell someone the truth that you observe:

- *Behaviors.* Since actions are observable, they are somewhat easier to confront. For example, a person in your life may be chronically late, never volunteer to help out, spend too much money, control others by intimidation, drink too much, or drive too fast.

- *Speech.* What we say tells a lot about who we are. You may be concerned about a friend's critical words, a tendency to turn conversations back to himself, silence and passivity, inappropriate laughter, or an inability to talk about personal matters, instead sticking with events and things.

• *Attitudes.* A little more difficult but perhaps the most important things to point out to someone you love, attitudes are about ways we look at life and relationships. Some examples of troublesome attitudes are a tendency to see others as less important than oneself, laziness, blaming others for problems, alternatively being too hard on oneself, and being negative about everything.

There are certainly many more examples within these categories. My point is that if you cover these three categories, you cover a lot of ground. Usually, however, we notice behaviors, speech, and attitudes because we encounter them in the relationship and *they bother us.* They bother us because *they should bother us.* These things get in the way of how life, love, and relationships should be conducted and carried out.

So if you notice harmful behaviors, speech, or attitudes in a loved one, simply bring it up to the person you love at an appropriate time by saying, "Can we talk about something?" I certainly know that when someone says that to me, it generally isn't going to be an affirmation or praise. It will be about a problem. But in my experience, the conversation has hardly ever been as bad as I anticipated, and it was very much worth it in what the person wanted to let me know. Realize that you are doing the person a favor, and bring it up.

TRUTH BRINGS RESOURCES

Sometimes awareness is not enough to solve the problem. Insight does not always cure, though it is necessary. There are many instances in which the person you care about may know about the problem but simply may not be able to overcome it. We cannot change everything about ourselves simply by trying harder or by willpower. If we could, we would not have needed God's grace in the first place. Here's how the apostle Paul describes this inner struggle: "I want to do what is good, but I don't. I don't want to do what is wrong, but I do it anyway. . . . Oh, what a miserable person I am! Who will free me from this life that is dominated by sin and death? Thank God! The answer is in Jesus Christ our Lord."[2]

All of us need to be aware of our situation, and many times we need help and resources to get out of it. As a loving person, then, you are not simply bringing the truth of awareness. You are bringing the truth and reality of good resources, which is extremely helpful and important.

For example, a friend of mine, Bob, who was single, told me he was struggling with Internet porn. Bob is a good guy, and he did not like what he was doing at all, but he could not stop. Awareness was not the issue with him; he was painfully aware of his situation. So we began to talk about how to help him. As he was someone I knew pretty well, I had been aware that he tended to withdraw emotionally when he was under stress or experiencing failure, both at work and in relationships. I remember a time when Bob's business had a huge downturn, and for months he did not mention to me how hard that was for him. So I hypothesized with him, "I wonder if part of the reason it's so difficult is that you use sex to self-medicate and comfort instead of asking for help."

> WE CANNOT CHANGE EVERYTHING ABOUT OURSELVES SIMPLY BY TRYING HARDER OR BY WILL POWER. IF WE COULD, WE WOULD NOT HAVE NEEDED GOD'S GRACE IN THE FIRST PLACE.

Bob is a reflective person, and after some thought, he said it made sense to him. Yet even though Bob had some awareness of his struggle, this awareness was not enough, and he knew it. So I said, "Why don't you have me and three other friends check in with you to see if you are checking in?" He looked confused. I continued. "In other words, if this pattern is due to your withdrawal from relationship, then get us to check to see if you are keeping us in the loop on your life and how you're doing. But I want you to call us, not us you. If we don't hear from you, we will call and say, 'Why aren't you calling us?'"

Bob was uncomfortable with my suggestion. He said, "I don't want to intrude; that sounds a bit extreme." I said, "It could be. Do you want to wait and keep doing what you are doing?" "No!" he said. "OK, I'll get some other buddies."

We set up the system. In a few weeks it was clear that Bob did have a habit of going to sex instead of addressing his struggles within relationships. Reaching out, asking for help, and trusting others were things he was afraid of

> SOMETIMES TELLING THE PERSON THE TRUTH MEANS SIMPLY TELLING HIM SOME THINGS THAT MIGHT HELP AND THEN BEING PART OF THE SOLUTION.

and did not do well. But he walked through the program and made very significant strides in his sexual control and purity.

My point is that sometimes telling the person the truth means simply telling him some things that might help and then being part of the solution. Bob was open to the information, and he was open, though less so, to the help. But it worked, and it works for most of us. So there is certainly a time for advice and suggestion, and this can be the place. After connection and awareness, sometimes a person just needs to hear an idea and have someone say, "I'm on the team, and I will help." Loving people tell the truth about helping and then put actions on the words. The structure and plans are often a big assistance.

TRUTH GETS PAST DEFENSES AND FEARS

There are times, however, when the person you love is not willing to look at his part in some problem. He is resistant. He is defensive. He makes excuses. He blames others, perhaps even you. He does not welcome the truth about himself but defends against it. So you, the loving person, are in a dilemma: You seek the person's best. You believe he has a problem that is hurting his life. But when you try to tell him the truth as you see it, he reacts negatively. Where do you go, and what do you do?

This is a very common problem, for all of us can be defensive at some point or another, some more and some less. There is little ground for superior or judging feelings here. By nature—that is, ever since Eve pointed at the serpent and Adam, being the more defensive of the couple, pointed at both Eve and God—we have resisted painful realities. There are different reasons for this. Some people are defensive because they have been hurt by judgment and are protecting themselves from further injury. Others resist reality because they simply have not had the experiences or training to know what to do with feedback. Another group wants something so badly that they don't want to see another side of things. And others do it because they possess an attitude that nothing is truly wrong with them, so it could not be them—or they may have what we call an entitlement problem, when the person feels entitled to special treatment for no good reason. They defend against the painful reality that that none of us deserves special treatment above another person.[3]

I was asked by some friends to help them with Martha, their elderly mom, whose driving ability had become a problem. Martha was a warm and loving person, and she had been a good driver for many years. But in the last few months, as happens with age, there had been enough scrapes, close calls, and incidents that it was clearly past the time to ask her to give up her keys.

I sat in the dining room with my friends as they tried to reason with her. They gave Martha the facts, the realities, their concerns. They talked about options, friends giving rides, bus systems, and elderly transit programs. They did a wonderful job of giving their mom lots of connection with the truth. I was quiet, not being sure as to what part I was to play.

Finally, Martha looked at me and said, "Can you reason with them? I need my independence."

I said, "I agree with them."

She didn't hear me correctly and said to her adult kids, "You see, at least someone is on my side."

I hated to say the next thing, but there was no other way to do it. I said to Martha, "No, I'm not on your side. I'm for you, and I care about you a lot, but I'm not on your side on this issue; I'm on your kids' side." I did not like the disappointment I saw on her face at all. But at the same time, I knew how deep her resistance was, and I knew I had to be clear so that more weight was added to her kids' perspective. And ultimately, Martha did surrender the keys and has adjusted very well to the new way of traveling. This mom was an example of someone being defensive because her independence and freedom was so important to her that she did not want to look at the other realities. And who could blame her?

Whatever the cause, defensiveness is a problem, and you, the loving person, need to learn what you can do to get past it. If you find yourself needing to tell the truth to someone who is resistant, here are some tips:

Find the right time and place. Defensiveness increases with stress and pressure; therefore it decreases with connection and peace. Be patient. Find or create a calm setting. Sometimes it even helps to make an appointment so that there will be no interruptions.

Come with care and humility. Start with letting the person know how much you value him or her and that you aren't perfect either. Perhaps you have even contributed to the problem. This eases the judgment fears that the person has.

Talk about the defensiveness. Sometimes, if you do not see any more willingness to take a look at things, it is helpful to bring the resistance out into the open. Let the person know how it may be affecting things and how you wish it could change. For example, suppose my conversation with Martha continued going the wrong way. I might have said, "It seems to me that maybe you're afraid of looking at the driving problem objectively because you value your independence so much. I understand that; freedom is important. But I am noticing that you aren't really listening to your children and what they are saying. I would like for you to put aside the need to drive, and please just be open to what they are saying."

This might have worked with Martha, perhaps not. In these situations, the other person always has a choice. But when defensiveness is getting in the way of life, love, or success, I think it is often helpful to make the person aware of it. There are some people who prefer to work around the defenses. That is, they try to figure a way to get the point in a manner that bypasses that person's resistance, for example, "Martha, I agree with you that independence is important and valuable. We want you to stop driving because it keeps you independent of having to worry about safety and accidents." While I can see that sometimes this is helpful, often I find it better to go for it, in as loving a way as possible. The defense is there. You and others can see it. And it will come up in other situations and be a negative thing for the person. I think it is better to help them talk about it so that they can learn to take ownership and responsibility for working through it and resolving it.

TRUTH HELPS HEAL DEEPER CHARACTER PROBLEMS

Then there are those situations in which the problem is not awareness, a need for resources, or resistance. Sadly, sometimes people do not care enough about how their problems affect their and others' lives. They have a character issue and brokenness that keeps them from being concerned about the hurts or struggles they contribute to in life, though they may be aware of it. These people are difficult to deal with. Yet they can benefit from your truth-telling love as well. Your loving confrontation with that person must be clear, direct, and sometimes accompanied by limits and consequences.

The issue with this sort of problem is that the person often is stunted or undeveloped in his ability to have empathetic care and compassion for others, being far more invested in his own point of view and experience. These people often have little value for honesty, and can easily deceive or manipulate things without feeling bad about it. For example, I knew a man named Mark who would be the nicest, funniest guy in the world when you saw him at church or at the kids' baseball games. But when he thought no one was looking, he would cruelly berate and harshly criticize his wife and kids. People would hear him in the car after a game, or coming out of their home, and it was very hurtful to his family. Eventually his wife got some help, and some friends confronted Mark with the truth about his behavior, in as loving a way as they could. They told him that though they cared about him, it was not OK, and never would be, to treat his family that way. They said they would take steps to help his family and to find help for him as well. I supported what they did.

Mark was enraged at what he called the judgment and condemnation of these people. He accused them of manipulating him, and the confrontation actually escalated his bad behavior with his family. Ultimately, he lost that family and, to my knowledge, is still blaming his wife and those friends for everything. Did they still do the right thing even when this was the result? I believe so. I believe not only was his family protected but he was given a gift of a direct and loving warning. I don't know if there was anything Mark's friends could have said that would have changed Mark. But they were loving, were clear, and provided solutions. Mark made the choice to continue in his ways.

At the same time, I have also seen that this sort of issue can greatly benefit the other person. I have seen other Marks who have responded well in these situations. Usually it takes a longer time than with other people and involves sometimes having to lose access to people or things that person wants, but the love, truth, and pressure can go a long way in helping the person turn around.[4]

CHECK YOUR MOTIVES

Since this is a book on helping you become a more loving person, it is very important that you have loving motives when you tell the truth. Our motives can drive a truth-telling conversation to a great resolution, resulting in change, closeness, perspective, and growth. Or they can bring things to an argument, cause alienation, or worse. So let's take an honest and real look at what is going on inside you.

IT IS VERY IMPORTANT THAT YOU HAVE LOVING MOTIVES WHEN YOU TELL THE TRUTH.

Why should we, and why do we, confront someone we care about? Your best and highest motive when you bring truth is that you are seeking the best for your loved ones. That is, you want them to succeed in life in all the important areas, such as relationships, family, work, and spirituality. You want them to solve problems. You desire for them to have a good life and become loving and responsible people. Basically, you want for them what you want for yourself. This is not always easy, especially when they bug you! But it is probably best to refrain from a confrontation until you have taken ownership of your motives.

The less helpful and darker motives do the opposite. They generally do not help others become better and can force them away from love, growth, and change. Here are some of the main motives we need to deal with.

REVENGE

Though no one likes to admit it, we often feel like hurting someone back who has hurt us. We want him to feel the pain he caused us. We want him to understand suffering the way we did. That is the motive of vengefulness or revenge. It is about punishment. It is certainly natural, but it is not mature or good for us.

Recently I confronted one of my sons about fooling around on the computer instead of studying. It was the right thing. He was not attending his studies. However, my tones and attitude were harsh with him, and he called me on it. He said, "I know I wasn't studying. But you came down too hard for what I was doing. I think it's because we had that argument about curfew during dinner." I thought about it. He was right. I was still mad about the argument, and it bled over into the computer problem. I told him, "You're right, I was still bugged and I should have been kinder with you with this issue. Sorry about that." Then we went on to deal with the computer problem, and I addressed it with the right amount of heat.

Do not assume you could never have vengeful motives. We all have a dark side, and the desire for revenge is universal. Entertain the thought that maybe the real reason you want to have a talk with the individual is because you're still mad at him. Let it go and give it up. As many preachers have said, "Revenge already got nailed to a bloodstained cross." Leave it on that cross, and get back to love.

RELIEF

Sometimes we are simply full of emotions and have nowhere to go with them, so we tell the truth to someone in order to get some relief for those feelings that are bottled inside. Sometimes this is called catharsis. Another way of looking at it is that we all need to confess. Confession is telling the truth about ourselves. And confession, especially emotional confession, helps us connect our feelings to others and bring them into relationship with people who care about us. Emotions were designed to be in relationship, and that is why we have the feeling of being bottled up until someone knows our feelings. Otherwise, the emotions grow too strong and we feel isolated and all alone with these intense, monstrous feelings inside.

> WE ALL NEED TO CONFESS. CONFESSION IS TELLING THE TRUTH ABOUT OURSELVES.

However, there is a right and a wrong way to connect and feel relief. The right way is often to get the person connected with someone else. That is, if you want the person you care about to feel open, safe, and ready to change, it may be a bad idea to blast the person emotionally, unless you are in a very healthy and resilient relationship. So get out what psychologists call the primitive material with a person who will listen, care, and help the feelings calm down and become less intense. We cannot always have everything we want, so give up the demand that the person hear all the negative emotional stuff—as well as thank you with open arms, be sorry, and change!

CONTROL

Love tells the truth, but love also protects the freedom of the other person. That includes his freedom to respond to your confrontation or to ignore it. That person has the choice, and you must be on the side of that choice, *even if it means choosing against you.* As soon as you try to make the other person listen or change, or insist on that, or manipulate the person to changing, or make him the bad guy because he does not agree, you have moved away from love.

Give up attempts to control and simply do what God does: ask, be vulnerable, reason, warn, and set limits if necessary. God always gives a choice. I have yet to find a Bible verse in which God says, "I'll make you love me." Instead, he says, "Hear me, obey me, follow me for these reasons." Erase the control motive from your life.

> THAT PERSON HAS THE CHOICE, AND YOU MUST BE ON THE SIDE OF THAT CHOICE, EVEN IF IT MEANS CHOOSING AGAINST YOU.

Here is what is most important to know about these and all other unhelpful motives: *they negate the value of the truth you have for the other person.* It is almost as if you had never said anything. People feel and experience your insides, and that speaks louder to them than your words. Do not make the mistake of justifying yourself here by saying, "Well, it's the truth." It may indeed be.

A mom may have just told her seven-year-old daughter how disappointed and sad her daughter made her when she acted up at the class party. That may be a fact, a reality. However, since most of the time parents say things like that to get some relief for their frustrations, instead of the parent dealing with it, the daughter will actually be more likely to either act up more, in defiance of being told to take responsibility for mom's feelings, or worse, disconnect and detach in guilt, becoming compliant so as not to upset her mom. Instead of negating the value of the truth, that mom could say, "You were disruptive, loud, and disobedient to your teacher at the party. I want that sort of behavior to stop, and I am going to give you a consequence so that you will remember to control yourself more next time." Now, with a clear and healthy motive, the truth can do its work.

TAKING THE NEXT STEPS

One of the most neglected aspects of being a loving person, truth is just an essential. Love is honest, and truth supports the purposes of love. Again, make sure your motives are to connect and help.

So grow and increase in your ability to connect and be honest. It is part and parcel of being loving. We cannot call ourselves truly loving unless we can tell the truth. Those who only connect run the risk of letting friends with serious problems be hurt further and hurt others. That is not truly seeking the best for the other. Go beyond good intentions, positive feelings, and intimacy. Be a truth-teller. Here are some tips to help:

- Talk about motives and approach with someone ahead of time. Get your safe people together and ask them to check your heart and motives. Then have them walk through what you will say to them. This will help you face and experience the anxiety and fear ahead of time and help you to push through it as you practice.[5]

- Give up the requirement for the person to like the truth and like you. Just as we learned that lovableness is no requirement for loving someone, neither is the other person wanting or appreciating the truth! It certainly goes better when the person you love is thankful and grateful. But sometimes that is not possible. If your loved one's life is going down the drain, someone needs to say something. Be that person.

- Be kind and direct. Keep grace and kindness first in the conversation as they help the medicine go down better. But don't dilute the truth or distract from it. I was at a seminar recently, teaching on honest relationships. Afterward, a woman came up to me and said, "The motto I learned is: 'Say what you mean, mean what you say, but don't say it mean.'" That is how I like to hear the truth, and that is how we need to dispense the truth!

- Own your contribution. Let the person you love know, early in the conversation, whatever you might have done to make the situation worse. This has several important benefits in loving people: it helps them hear what you have to say because it shows you care; it makes it sound less superior and judging; and we need to do it for our own benefit. Remember Jesus' words: "First get rid of the log in your own eye; then you will see well enough to deal with the speck in your friend's eye."[6] Tell the person if you were afraid to say something, or if you were silently resentful, or if you condemned him passively. Apologize and move on.

- Ask for specific changes. People need the grace of clarity. It is not easy to hear truth. Hearing truth that you have no idea how to respond to is immensely difficult. Give the person a path, direction, and steps to take. For example, notice the differences in the truth statements below: "I want you to connect more with me and stop hiding behind the computer." This is truth, but it is global and vague. And it's hard to know whether you have done this or not. "I need time with you every day if possible where I have your full attention, eye contact, and we talk about our lives, stresses, and each other. When is a good time for you?" This gives the person a structure and direction. People you love may actually want to love you back! But they will need your help in how they can love you.

- Stay with your definition of love. When you confront a loved one with the truth, you may get a negative reaction, and you may be accused of being mean or unloving. If you and your friends have already cleared out your motives, don't let the attack get you off balance. Remember your definition of love. You are seeking the best for the other. Your truth-telling may have nothing to do with what the other person thinks is loving. But it may have a lot to do with what God and reality say is loving.

- Make truth as normal and natural as connection. Take steps in your daily life to be more honest. Not mean, but authentic and truthful. Surround yourself with honest people. Make telling your reality a normal function of your life. Truth-telling should not be the aberration in love and relationships. The absence of truth-telling should be the aberrant behavior. Be the sane one and love people with the truth!

My experience is that there are three types of individuals you will encounter when you love people as a truth-teller. One group will appreciate your truthfulness and support you. They will move toward you, love you back, and make it safe for you to be honest with them and vice versa.

The second type will resist and get mad. It is good to know this so you understand their character and will know how to deal with them. Don't set yourself up for harm or danger, but at the same time, see what effect truth has on them.

And the third group of people are in the middle: they are new to all this, and it feels uncomfortable, but they are good-hearted and open to the value of truth. Stay with them, show them what you are learning, and get them on the team! We need more loving people in this world who are competent connectors and effective confronters.

FIVE

Healing: Restoring the Broken

Recently I spoke at a seminar on relationships and growth. During the breaks, I chatted with people and signed books. As I talked to the attendees, I began to hear a pattern in what they said to me as I met them. They mentioned a woman named Beth. And they would make statements about Beth's influence on their personal growth and healing process. These statements stand out to me:

"Beth teaches your materials in our growth group and has helped me so much."

"Beth is the reason I came today."

"I am a different person because of a woman named Beth."

"I was in Beth's group years ago, and now I am leading my own group."

"You have to meet Beth; she changed my life."

Yes, I thought, *I have to meet Beth!* When I was introduced to her, I quickly got it about her. I was drawn to who she was as a person. We spent awhile talking about her own growth and development process, for she was clearly into spiritual, emotional, and personal change. Beth is one of those easy-to-love people. Her care for people, her character, her depth, and her sense of humor were all a warm combination. She told me that she has been leading small groups on growth for many years, and it is what she loves most.

Here is the significant part: Beth is not a formally trained therapist or clinician. Nor is she a pastor or a pastoral counselor. Yet person after person attribute much of their own healing and growth to Beth. Why is this? Because Beth is a loving person, and she has *learned how to use love in a way that heals and restores people who struggle or are in pain.* She is competent and puts her whole being into the process. And the fruit she is bearing is now entering new generations.

I have met many people like Beth, and they are some of my favorite people in the world. They are living regular lives, with regular jobs and relationships. And they are deeply touching and impacting lives in ways that truly make a difference. The reality is that all loving people can become a part of and engage in the process of healing and growth. It is not a gift reserved for the few; it is an integral and important part of loving people in a way that seeks their best.

HEALING AND LOVE

A discussion on healing may seem out of place in a book on love. After all, this is not intended to be a counseling or recovery or self-help book. It is simply about becoming a more loving person, in the best sense of the word, and to be seeking and doing what is best for another. But it does fit, because the reality of brokenness is such a large part of the lives of the people you love. You cannot separate our lives from the hurts we experience. The need for restoring people to wholeness is huge and present and universal.

ALL LOVING PEOPLE CAN BECOME A PART OF AND ENGAGE IN THE PROCESS OF HEALING AND GROWTH.

Think for a moment about the struggles you see in people you know and care about. You are likely very close to friends and family who have hurts and baggage. Statistics say that it is likely that you are also on this list. It is normal to suffer. It is normal to have issues that get in the way of life. It is normal to experience some form of what we call brokenness. That is the heritage we have from living in a fallen world that has gotten lost in self-sufficiency and distance from God's plan. Loving people are actively involved in doing what is best to help others heal and mend.

Personal brokenness is an inner issue—that is, it comes from something inside us that is not working right. But it manifests itself in visible, measurable ways. Basically, there are three areas in which people experience symptoms that point to a deeper issue to become aware of and resolve: clinical, relational, and functional. Remember, however, that these three areas are the fruit, not the root, of our brokenness.

CLINICAL SYMPTOMS

The term *clinical* means that the problem is either severe enough or complex enough that it requires some professional intervention to resolve it. Just as a fever may not be a clinical issue unless it spikes to a dangerous level because an infection is behind it, so also are emotional and behavioral problems. Depression, anxiety disorders, addictions, substance abuse, eating disorders, and compulsive disorders are examples from the clinical world. As we will see during this chapter, you may be surprised at the extent and depth of help you can provide on a nonprofessional level to people you care about who have clinical issues.

RELATIONAL SYMPTOMS

We live and operate in relationships: our family, loved ones, friends, colleagues, and spiritual attachments are all part of what life is about for us. When we struggle internally, it is common for relational breakdowns to be the result. Healthy relationships work best with the building blocks of two healthy people. But when an individual has something wrong inside, it is more difficult to connect, be vulnerable, solve problems, and grow together. Some examples of relational symptoms are alienation of love, control problems, harmful criticism, irresponsibility, self-centeredness, abandonment, deception, and unfaithfulness.

FUNCTIONAL SYMPTOMS

Much of what we do in life is literally that: *what we do.* I am referring to the tasks of our lives in which we are involved in effort—the creative process, accomplishments, and the like. Some examples of problems in the functional realm are work and career struggles, difficulties reaching goals and dreams, problems completing projects and tasks, issues with focus and concentration, and the inability to clearly know how to invest our time, talents, and treasures in some meaningful way. It is common for a businessperson to become aware that he has a brokenness issue through the reality of a work problem that will not go away no matter how hard he tries.

So the human race is in a mess! However, as the architect of love and of restoring the human race, God has placed love squarely in the middle of the healing process. It is the central and most significant element of what helps people get their lives back together, transform their emotions and behaviors, and put the pieces of their hearts into something that works and makes sense. God's love, in the person of Jesus, had restoration in the announcement of the purpose of his coming: "The Spirit of the LORD is upon me, for he has anointed me to bring Good News to the poor. He has sent me to proclaim that captives will be released, that the blind will see, that the oppressed will be set free."[1] And as his followers and representatives, we are to follow that calling.

> **LOVING PEOPLE ARE ACTIVELY INVOLVED IN DOING WHAT IS BEST TO HELP OTHERS HEAL AND MEND.**

Just to clarify terms, connecting, as I discussed in Chapter 3, is not identical to healing. Though connecting is a necessary element of healing, connecting is broader in focus, while healing is narrower. A way to understand the distinction is that connecting can serve many purposes: the need to get out of isolation, joy, personal growth, and so forth. But the healing part of love has one central focus, and that is to assist someone in repairing some injury, wound, or issue that they cannot do for themselves. Not only that, but healing also involves other efforts besides connection that work together to help the process move along.

AN OPEN DOOR

A psychologist friend and I were talking about the counseling process. He mentioned a book I had written and suggested that it had too much emphasis on small groups and not enough emphasis on counseling. I thought a long time about what my colleague said because he is a good and perceptive person. However, I concluded that I did not agree with him.

I certainly have great value and faith in all the good that professional psychology and trained therapists have accomplished over the years. Their expertise, depth of understanding of the human heart, and compassion can bring life-changing transformation to the suffering that people experience. I have been involved in clinical work for a long time and have seen its effectiveness.

And there is a great deal of healing that can best be done by people formally trained in counseling. The amount of information, experience, and learning involved simply takes that sort of time. For example, there are types of depressions that can look identical in their symptoms, such as withdrawal, painful emotions, hopeless thinking, and problems in sleeping and eating. Yet they can have quite different causes: the inability to make an emotional attachment, experiencing a profound loss, problems in being a separate person, perfectionistic strivings, and trauma. The training provides the ability to diagnose the cause, and knowing the cause allows the clinician to know the treatment, because the treatment is different for each cause. Then the counseling process itself is complex, involving dealing with internal distortions of one's view of oneself, others, and the world, developmental injuries, cognitive problems, inabilities to regulate emotions, conscience conflicts, and so forth. So the point is, just as you would want to see a surgeon for surgery, a mechanic for an auto problem, and a computer expert for your PC, you should see a trained clinician for emotional and medical issues that require that level of training.

Having said that, however, I also believe that individuals who are not therapists can do a phenomenal amount of good in the healing process. There is much that a loving person can accomplish with understanding and experience. And that is what I would like for you to know about. You, if you are a layperson and want to help, should understand all the good you can do and how much brokenness you can mend in the lives of people who need it. You have an open door of opportunity to make a difference in significant ways.

Loving people are the primary agents of restoration. That is the way it has been since time began. We are the stewards of grace toward each other, and the grace we provide for each other simply makes things better. Every day, people who care are bringing healing, change, and transformation to individuals in their lives.

Let me give you a personal example. Recently I was speaking at a seminar, and the morning before I was to speak, I was reading my Bible in the hotel room. I read in Genesis 22 where God took Abraham through the ultimate test of being willing to give up his son, Isaac. I thought about what that might mean for me, and one idea that occurred was obvious, because my wife and I

LOVING PEOPLE ARE THE PRIMARY AGENTS OF RESTORATION.

have two teenage sons. What made it worse was that now they are both driving, which is nerve-racking for any parent. So it bothered me a little. But I figured that maybe the message for me had to do with something broader, such as being willing to have faith in God no matter the circumstances. I said a prayer and left to speak at the seminar.

After the morning sessions I met with the leaders of the event for lunch. One of the leaders was talking about some subject I now cannot remember, but to illustrate her point, she mentioned the story of Tony Dungy, Super Bowl–winning coach of the Indianapolis Colts. She talked about his faith in God, even in the face of the tragic death of his son, James.

Immediately my stomach dropped, and I began to feel strong anxiety and dread. I did feel compassion for Tony Dungy's grief, but at the same time I could not help thinking, *Is God preparing me for the unthinkable? Why am I hearing his story just a few hours after reading that passage?* When the lunch ended and it was time for me to continue the seminar, I knew I was actually in some trouble. I went to Ken, a pastor friend of mine who was leading the event, and asked him for a few minutes alone before I spoke. When we got in a room by ourselves, I told Ken what was going on. I said that I had no idea about what the real meaning of any of this was, but I knew that was not the point right now. I just did not want to be alone with these feelings before I spoke, both for my sake and the audience's. I was afraid that these strong feelings would affect the talk in a bad way. He said he was available to help in any way he could. So I just let the feelings out. I cried and experienced my sudden terror about my sons. Ken stayed with me, being kind, empathizing and praying for me. I knew he was present and that he got it, and he helped me tolerate the feelings I could not tolerate by myself. Within a couple of minutes the intensity was gone and I was ready to finish the day, which proceeded normally.

That process was healing for me. I was in great emotional pain and could not manage it alone. Ken's presence and steadiness did the job for me. He is not a counseling pastor; he works in other areas of his profession. But he was available, he cared, and he showed up with grace. That is what I mean by how much we can do for each other. You, as a loving person, can be a Ken for people you love.

Another aspect of healing is that you can also be part of the support system or network for a person going through a clinical issue. Emotional growth and healing are almost always strengthened and deepened when the person in counseling has people in his life who are doing their part in the process. When an individual who is depressed or has a major loss or an addiction is involved with a good small group, or even a set of friends who know the problem and want to help, this does several things for him. It gives him other avenues of grace and acceptance besides the counselor. It provides reinforcement for the learning experiences the person is dealing with in the office. It breaks up the week into smaller segments so that the person does not have to go a long time without having someone to talk to. It provides a foundation so that he is more stable and secure. Sometimes when I am working with a client, and if it is clinically appropriate and the client gives written permission, I will talk to some significant people in his life and give them guidelines on how they can be a help to his growth and healing.

YOU CAN ALSO BE PART OF THE SUPPORT SYSTEM OR NETWORK FOR A PERSON GOING THROUGH A CLINICAL ISSUE.

For example, I worked with Will, a man who had been unfaithful to his wife, Amy, and whose life was falling apart. Amy was of course devastated, and she almost ended the marriage. But she decided to stay and see if Will could really change and if she could trust him again, for she was a good person, and she did love him. On his part, Will was authentic in his remorse and concern over what he had done to Amy, and he told me he would do whatever it took to resolve what influenced him to be unfaithful. That was the right thing to say, and Will really meant it. He began to face and own what he had done. We uncovered issues that created a vulnerability toward seeking out other women. Will also took responsibility for his anger at Amy and his lies and his duplicity with her. He began putting the pieces together of why he would be so destructive toward her. It was very painful work, but it was bearing good fruit.

During our time in counseling, Will told me that his small group, one he had been in for a long time and with whom he was very attached, had volunteered to help in any way they could with his process, and they wanted to know if I would provide guidelines. I liked the fact that they didn't reject him and instead wanted to come alongside him. Many other friends had left him, and Will had to deal with those losses. I talked to Will about this for a while, because my first responsibility and concern was his treatment, and I didn't want anything disrupting that. I especially didn't want Will having difficulties trusting me because I had been in contact with others in his life, not being sure what I might say. Trust is a foundation of the therapeutic process, and it takes time and work to establish. That is why the confidentiality laws governing psychotherapy, which protect the client's privacy, are so strict. They have to be, for the well-being of the client.

I evaluated Will's character makeup, his issues, any fragilities he might have, and where he was in his treatment to determine the effects of talking to his friends. Then I worked with him on his own feelings and desires about his small group being involved. I didn't want him to do this to keep them happy, nor to manipulate their feelings toward him. But it turned out that, while he wanted some control over what I would divulge, he sincerely wanted his small group to have my input. I consulted a colleague about the possible risks, and, after thinking and talking through it, she agreed that she didn't think it would be harmful, and it could help a great deal, given the situation. I finally made the determination that this would do no harm to Will if handled correctly. And it could assist his healing. Most of the time I do not do this because of the possible complications. But the situation, circumstances, and aspects of the case seemed safe to me as I evaluated and sought consultation.

At that point, Will and I crafted the things his small group could do to help him grow and change. He then signed releases for me to talk to the members, with limits set up on the documents, of what I could and could not discuss with them. And that is the point of all this, because what we came up with are things that you, as a loving person who wants to help in healing, can do. Here are a few of the recommendations:

- To continue to meet during the regular small group times. Will needed the structure and the regularity of knowing there was a place he could go where he could process what was going on.

- To assure him that they were for him—that is, while they thought the affair was wrong, he was a member of their group; so they loved, forgave, and were deeply committed to him.

- To be safe for him: It was OK for him to talk about the issue and unpack it with them. They were attached enough, and resilient enough, to handle it and help him process it.

- To pray with him and help him in his own spiritual confession and repentance process.

- To let Will know how the deception affected them personally. What feelings did they have about him showing up at group week after week and not being honest about the nightmare in which he was living? They had their own hurt, anger, and trust issues, and it was important that Will face those with them.

- To be a place where he would be accountable in other areas of his life to be honest, especially those which had contributed to the affair. For example, Will tended to withdraw when he was hurt or angry, rather than open up or confront. This was a big part of why the affair started. He chose acting out over bringing his negative feelings to Amy. The group was to encourage him to be truthful about negative things with him and to confront him when they saw him pulling away or being indirect.

- To help him take risks to be a better person and to see him through those risks. The first time Will got really angry in group with one of the members, he started yelling, and it got intense. He had never been this truthful before, as his "nice guy" facade had always been intact. The group stayed with him, listened to him, and helped him deal with and experience his anger. He became more comfortable with speaking up and letting people know his real feelings.

- To help him not blame Amy but instead see how what he did affected her; therefore he would have compassion for her own pain.

- To not let his issues take over the group, so that the members wouldn't have time to talk about their own lives. Rather, the idea was that he was just another group member, showing up, interacting about the study materials, talking about his life and listening to theirs, giving and receiving personal feedback, and praying together. This helped him feel normal and not like a freak in the group.

The group entered into the process, and, after I had the initial talk with them, I backed out and resumed treatment with Will. He would report to me what had happened in his small group meetings. And it really helped. The work they were doing with him was consistent with the work he and I were doing. They were good people, and they made a difference. And I could see the changes and transformations in Will as he moved into becoming a new, loving, honest, healed person and husband. This structure helped him make significant strides.

As you look at the group's participation with Will, think of yourself. Most likely you would be able to do most of the things the group did. The group did what people do who care and are involved with someone who is broken and starting to heal. And probably you would want an opportunity to do these things. There is real power and effectiveness when the body of Christ has a chance and a structure to do what it is supposed to do with its members.

THE ELEMENTS OF LOVE THAT HEALS

I would like to break down for you what abilities and skills you will need to have or to acquire in order to be not just a connector and a truth-teller but also a healer. There are several categories of these elements of healing.

RECEIVE HEALING AND PERSONAL GROWTH FOR YOURSELF

If you have experienced the help and power of participating in the healing process, you have head knowledge and personal experience of what healing is about. Most schools of psychology require therapy for their students. Many seminaries and other traditions also encourage their students to receive counseling. This is not only for the benefit of the student, because everyone has something to work on, but also to understand the process on a level that cannot be done in any other way.

You may not have ever considered getting help for yourself, whether in a professional or lay capacity. But think about how your life is going in relationship, family, love, work, habits, and behaviors. Consider your past experiences in significant relationships and their effects on your present days. Most of us can identify things that trouble us, which we have attempted to improve or correct but have not been able to see the progress we would like so far. There are many healthy and helpful counselors, therapists, spiritual directors, mentors, small groups, and churches available for you and for those you want to help.

God is the initiator of a process of comfort that trickles down to all of us. I encourage you to receive God's comfort so you can give it to others: "He comforts us in all our troubles so that we can comfort others. When they are troubled, we will be able to give them the same comfort God has given us."[2]

GET MENTORING AND TRAINING IN HEALING

Next to your own healing, there is no better element for this aspect of being a loving person than getting instruction and training in helping the brokenness of others. Spending time with an experienced person who can navigate the waters of the human heart has great value. Fortunately, many organizations and churches have training programs that will go from several months to a few years, usually meeting weekly. They can be very helpful. Also, some people will one-on-one spend time with a professional therapist just to get nonclinical supervision, and that has great benefits as well. In fact, when you finish your training, I suggest you stay in some sort of mentor or supervisory relationship as long as you are working with others. They can see things you might miss and can keep you from making mistakes.

CONNECT WITH A FOCUS

Remember all the principles and tips you read about connecting in Chapter 3? They apply here, as good healers must be good connectors. However, there is a particular direction and focus of the connection, and that is *the connection moves toward pain*. When people struggle in relationship, feelings, or behaviors, they almost always have some experienced pain inside, and not much can happen until that is brought into the connection. The pain must be identified, brought into relationship, and understood.

That pain may not be the source of the problem. In fact, it may be a symptom of the problem. For example, a person suffering from a particular type of depression may feel intense guilt for some real or perceived transgression.

NEXT TO YOUR
OWN HEALING,
THERE IS NO
BETTER ELEMENT
FOR THIS ASPECT
OF BEING A
LOVING PERSON
THAN GETTING
INSTRUCTION AND
TRAINING IN
HELPING THE
BROKENNESS OF
OTHERS.

However, the guilt may cover up anger at some injury or mistreatment, which she then turns on herself, creating the guilt, which then contributes to the depression. In this instance, the pain of the guilt may be the symptom, but the pain of the prohibited anger is more of the source. The point is, however, that she needs someone to connect with the pain she experiences in order to get to the source of the problem. So in this situation the person needs you to listen and have empathy for the guilt she feels.

If you are to move toward pain, it makes sense that you need to be able to tolerate it in someone. People in the healing process certainly need a path and a solution, and those are there. But they often try to get to the path without fully understanding the strength of their negative feelings; therefore attempting to skip that step. I don't blame them for that. But if they do not feel what they need to feel, they run the risk of returning to those feelings again later when you are not around. Sometimes they aren't avoiding pain. They simply aren't aware that the painful emotions exist. So they must rely on others to help them become aware of, and also connect, those experiences. As a loving person who wants to heal, you are to get past the tendency we have to avoid the negative, move toward the positive, and provide advice.

Recently I was facilitating a group of leaders who wanted to grow personally as well as professionally. Leaders have a particular pressure on them to be positive, to provide vision and encouragement. It is sometimes difficult for leaders to move toward others' pain, as well as their own. Their training makes this counterintuitive for them. During our sessions, I noticed that Hal, one of the participants, would be too positive too quickly in this manner. For example, Robin, another group member, began opening up about her troubled marriage and the emptiness and sadness she felt, as well as how it affected her leadership role in the business she was in. It was new for her to talk about this openly, and she was experiencing lots of emotions about it. The rest of the group was attentive, leaning in to Robin's sadness and encouraging her to bring them into her hurting world. But in the middle of this, Hal said, "I know it's going to be OK for you. God has a plan in all this, and things may not even be as bad right now as you think they are. What lessons do you think you are learning from all this?"

> IF YOU ARE TO MOVE TOWARD PAIN, IT MAKES SENSE THAT YOU NEED TO BE ABLE TO TOLERATE IT IN SOMEONE.

I have no doubt that Hal meant well, for he is a good person, and he really cared about the woman. But he was not helping Robin heal. I said, "Hal, I am glad you want to help Robin. But you are coming up with the happy ending for her too soon. These feelings and parts of her have never been connected in relationship. Until they are, she can't do much to transform them. So I need for you to stay with her dark present, not the happy ending, until she knows we understand." Hal responded well and became more empathetic. Robin was helped, and she eventually was able to come up with a plan to improve her marriage that was based on what she had experienced with the group.

So use the pain as your guide, and connect in that manner. Here are some things you can say that will help:

- "That must have been difficult."

- "Sounds like you got hurt in that relationship."

- "I can see that you really beat yourself up when you do that."

- "I know you say it's OK, but your face looks sad.
  Is it still bothering you?"

- "Tell me more about how it feels."

- "I'm really sad for how tough this is."

- "I'd be angry too."

You can see that these statements are geared toward going deeper, where the person is suffering. This can do worlds of good. Being able to have someone else go there with them, stay with them, and scour the issue and the feelings will bring them relief and free them from the intensity and aloneness they may feel, and they will be able to move on to the next step. Most of the time there is more to do in the healing process. But do not be afraid of staying with the feelings. Remember the timing: advice and wisdom generally come after hearing and understanding. "He who answers before listening—that is his folly and his shame."[3]

> REMEMBER THE TIMING: ADVICE AND WISDOM GENERALLY COME AFTER HEARING AND UNDERSTANDING.

ADDRESS DEFLECTION

Be attentive also to the reality that the person who is struggling may unknowingly move away from the connection. It is common for individuals to avoid pain or feel bad about taking up others' time. Or they may be afraid of bringing you down. So look for changes such as losing eye contact, changing the subject back to you, coming up with premature positive statements, and the like. Say, "When you started talking about your illness and what that may be doing to your career, I really felt how scary that was for you. But then when you said, 'So how is your job?' to me, I couldn't hang with you as well. I really want to know how difficult this is for you, if you want to continue talking about it."

HOLD ON TO YOUR OWN REALITY

People who hurt need someone who will connect but still be separate and their own person. It helps them for you to be able to empathize and yet have your own perspective, feelings, and opinions. That makes the process safer for them, for they are often afraid that the intense sadness, guilt, anger, or fear will contaminate others and overwhelm them the way they are overwhelming the other person. Be stronger than their feelings. It is easy for healers to get lost in the experience of another person, and that is OK for brief periods of time for purposes of identification and understanding. But be sure to return to your own thoughts and viewpoint, as the person you are helping needs that strength, objectivity, and stability from you.

NOTICE WHEN THE PAIN MAY BE TOO MUCH, AND STOP

One word of warning here: sometimes if a person has some fragility or damage in an area, it isn't good for the person to stay with too much pain for too long. In some instances, the person can begin to feel more hopeless or discouraged and go backward, because he doesn't have enough love or structure inside to deal with it in large doses. He may need to have a systematic approach of being strengthened, then going deeper, then more strengthening, and so forth. So if you and the person notice that things are getting worse, get him to someone with clinical training who can help him safely do this.

PROVIDE CONSTANCY AND STRUCTURE

Individuals who are in the healing process need the bridge of focused connection. But they also need someone who can provide structure, reality, and constancy for them. When people hurt, they often feel that their lives are unreal or upside down, or that things make no sense. Having people in their lives who are steady, nonreactive, responsible, reliable, and realistic can go a long way toward helping them tolerate and heal.

Do not miss the importance of this aspect of healing, for it is profound. One of the conclusions of research with trauma survivors, from World War II to Vietnam to 9/11, is the need for a predictable order of life for those people. If they are able, and not so damaged that they cannot function, one of the best things for them is to return to work and to their usual habits and routines. It helps them begin re-creating a sense of normalcy when events have indicated that normal doesn't exist for them anymore.

As a loving person, you can help the healing when you do some of the things listed below:

- Set up regular meeting and phone call times.

- Be dependable: show up on time, and end things on time.

- Support their return to routine, and help them to get back to it.

- When they have strong feelings, don't get caught up in them. Listen to them, understand, but be the stable one.

- Provide common sense and advice that supports responsible living.

- If they get impulsive, ask them to wait on any big decisions.

- Be reasonable and realistic.

This is what friends have done for friends throughout the ages. It is not magic. But it is a very effective part of love and healing. As a proverb says, "Many will say they are loyal friends, but who can find one who is truly reliable?"[4]

HELP IDENTIFY CAUSES AND UNDERLYING ISSUES

When people have a personal struggle, the problem is generally not the problem. That is, most of the time when people have some struggle or difficulty that is causing them to want to talk to you about it, there is something else driving it. The pain is, more often than not, a symptom of the problem.

OFTENTIMES, THOSE WHO NEED HEALING ALSO NEED HELP IN IDENTIFYING THE ROOTS.

Pain serves to alert the individual that there is something broken that must be attended to. That is, in fact, its purpose. As C. S. Lewis said, "Pain is God's megaphone."[5] Relational struggles, anxieties, eating problems, sexual issues, and depressions usually are a fruit of something going on in the person's life and character. Oftentimes, those who need healing also need help in identifying the roots.

Take weight issues, for example. We all know by now that the only way to lose weight and keep it off is some combination of diet and exercise. However, in many cases, that is not all that is needed, as there are emotional parts to the equation too. A friend of mine, Pam, who was struggling with her weight, asked me for help, not as a therapist but as a friend. She had every diet book in the world and a gym membership. Pam was in the typical discouraging yo-yo pattern, in which she would lose a few pounds, get encouraged, then binge and gain it all back. She said, "I just need to be more disciplined and stick to the plan."

"Sure," I said. "Your plan sounds fine. But I don't think you can just choose to stick to it more."

"What do you mean?"

I said, "How long have you been working on the plan without it working for you?"

Pam sighed. "OK, years."

"So I don't think more dedication and commitment will do. I think there is something else keeping you from the plan."

"Like what?" she asked.

"I don't know," I said. "But there are lots of ways of finding out. For example, you might try keeping a three-by-five card around for a couple of weeks, and every time you binge, write down what was going on in your life and emotions just before you started eating. That's one way."

"Maybe I just get hungry," Pam said.

"I doubt it. The yo-yo pattern indicates that this is conflict within: part of you wants to get in shape, and part is having a struggle."

Pam and I talked a few weeks later. She had an "aha moment" after a few days. She explained, "I found something like a pattern in the overeating with this three-by-five card thing. Whenever I have a disagreement with someone important to me, or they are disappointed with me, I feel horrible and I eat. It happened with my husband and my son this week."

"Let's pursue that," I said. "Why do you feel horrible when people are at odds with you?"

"It's like they hate me, and I'm no good."

"OK, we're getting somewhere. Why would your husband's disappointment in you make you feel so extremely bad?"

And we took it from there.

As the conversation continued, Pam began to see what was happening. She was not separate and distinct enough from the people in her life. Like a chameleon takes on the colors of its surroundings, Pam took on the perspective of those around her. (Actually, no one thought that poorly of her. She magnified their negative reactions to an unrealistically harsh degree.) So, feeling so bad about herself because she couldn't distance from their feelings, she turned to food. Eating was something that she could control and that she had some choices about. Eating didn't make her lose herself. This was a helpful awareness for Pam, for it gave her a path to a root cause. She began working on owning her own feelings, being clear about her experiences, saying no, confrontation, and the like. Within a short amount of time, she worked through it, and the weight plan worked as it was supposed to for her.

> PART OF BEING A HEALER IS BEING ABLE TO GO BEYOND THE SYMPTOMS TO WHAT IS ACTUALLY BROKEN IN THE PERSON'S LIFE AND HEART.

Pam's experience provides a good example for anyone who wants to heal: when people come to you with a struggle, help them to look deeper inside for a cause. If they have had a struggle for a long time, either there is something else underneath, or they don't have the resources they need, or they are avoiding taking ownership. You can do a lot to help people this way.

Here are some of the underlying issues that drive many emotional and personal struggles. The important thing to understand is that these different issues may result in very similar problems, symptoms, patterns, or bad fruit in a person's life. This is similar to what I said earlier about how different causes can form almost identical symptoms of depression.

Part of being a healer is being able to go beyond the symptoms to what is actually broken in the person's life and heart. Keep these in mind as you listen and connect:

- *Isolation and detachment.* We were designed by God to be in relationship with him and with each other. Most of the elements of our survival and success come from relationships. So when there is a breakdown in the ability to trust, open up, need, and connect, the elements do not come our way and we have no access to what we need for life. The result is often psychological, emotional, or relational brokenness.

- *Boundary and responsibility problems.* When we are not clear about who we are and what we will allow, we will not have control over our lives or choices in our relationships, as was the situation in Pam's case. Often, people with boundary struggles will get caught up in rescuing and enabling others, will suffer with guilt issues, and will experience problems in burnout, performance issues, and lack of focus.

- *The inability to deal with reality.* The reality is that of imperfection: the imperfection of ourselves, others, and the world. We all need to be able to live in the awareness of these imperfections, but often we cannot because it is hard to look at and experience. The result is that we experience shame, perfectionistic tendencies, self-judgment, self-absorption, and defensiveness. These then readily lead to depressions, conflicts in love, and fear of failure at work, for a few examples.

- *Difficulty in taking adult control of our lives.* At some point, we are to move from childhood dependency to adult maturity. This means being in charge of our lives, our talents, our sexuality, how we deal with authority, and how we handle the disapproval of others. When people are stuck in this process, they will sometimes have trouble with overcompliance or chronic rebellion with authority figures, sexual conflicts, or fears of criticism.

- *Trauma.* When a person experiences some catastrophic, violent, or abusive event, it is sometimes beyond their ability to absorb, digest, deal with, and move on. They will often replay the event without end or have it come out in symbolic fashions in their relationships.

- *Ungrieved losses.* Losing a loved one, our health, an opportunity, a job, or money can cause emotional and personal struggles too. Losses were meant to be grieved, but often people don't know how to go about this.

- *Medical difficulties.* It is always wise to make sure anyone you care about who needs healing has had a medical checkup. Many clinical, relational, and functional problems can be caused by health issues, ranging from hormone problems, biochemical imbalances, diabetes, or organ breakdowns.

The point here is simply to make sure you are helping people look beyond the pain to what might be causing the pain. One of the things I see often is someone who wants to help but finds himself simply comforting pain over and over again while the pain continues to resurface. The root cause or issue is not touched, so there is an endless cycle of difficulty with no end in sight. Instead, help your loved one get to the source of the pain so the person can get it resolved.

PROVIDE AND BECOME A RESOURCE

People who are in the healing process need more than compassion and understanding. They also need resources to resolve and become whole again. Part of them is missing, undeveloped, or injured. They generally need some supplies for what they either lost or never had in the first place. Let me illustrate: Suppose an individual finds herself continually controlled by toxic people in her life—the wrong sorts of men, or family members who manipulate her, or a dominating work relationship. She may understand clearly that it is not the people who are the problem but rather her giving these people power—and in some cases actually seeking these sorts of people out. She may know that it isn't good for her. She may truly want to make better choices in relationships and to establish more boundaries in the relationships she has.

But she needs more than these insights. She needs to be strengthened inside so that she can actually do this. She needs people to resource her in several ways. For example, she needs:

- grace to know that she is loved and valued no matter what;

- assurance that if she becomes honest and says no to controlling people and gets a bad reaction from them, she will not be alone and isolated from people who love her;

- experiences with individuals she can confess her fears and guilt to, with no shame about it;

- safe ways she can disagree with people who will respect and move toward her, not away from her;

- accountability to push ahead and face her fears when she avoids the issues;

• confrontation when she rationalizes or blames;

• feedback on how you perceive her and how she affects you; and

• practice sessions where she can role-play confrontive conversations so that she experiences and pushes through her anxiety.

Now you have become a resource for her. You are part of her redemptive support system. You are changing her life with her. To the best of your ability, take an active role in giving people the love and experiences they need for growth and repair.

However, you cannot do it all, nor should you attempt to. People who need healing generally need other resources. For example, they may need a professional therapist for a situation that requires it. So make sure you can refer and suggest other people, groups, and sources of information

PEOPLE WHO NEED HEALING GENERALLY NEED OTHER RESOURCES.

besides yourself that apply to the person's situation. Do some research and find out where the experts, churches, and mentors in that particular area are. Be a bridge, a conduit. Loving people pour life inside others, and they also point the way to other sources of life.

BE PATIENT WITH THE PROCESS

You will do a world of healing when you allow the person in your life ample time to change and heal. My experience in this area is that it usually takes longer to heal than anyone thought at the outset of the process. Healing is hard work! They will have setbacks, resistances, fears, denial, and life problems that will distract them. Do not be impatient or frustrated with them. Think about your own life and how many steps backward you have taken.

Psychologists have researched how the process of change works, and there are several identified stages of change.[6] There is the precontemplation stage in which the individual isn't sure they have an issue that needs resolving or healing. They know something may be wrong, but they are still thinking about it or are not yet ready to face the reality. There is the contemplation stage in which they understand there is something wrong but have not taken any steps yet.

They know they have an emotional, behavioral, or relational brokenness, but they are still mustering courage to take some risks. There is the action stage in which they enter the process and actually talk to someone or join a growth setting. And there is the maintenance stage in which they have made some successes and want the progress to continue over time.

IF YOU ARE TOO FAR AHEAD OF PEOPLE, YOU RISK LOSING THEM. YOU NEED TO BE RIGHT THERE WITH THEIR THINKING, HELPING THEM GET TO THE NEXT STAGE.

The stages of change research provides an important takeaway for you who want to help: *if you are too far ahead of people, you risk losing them.* You need to be right there with their thinking, helping them get to the next stage. Don't be two stages ahead and expect them to catch up. It rarely happens. They are likely to be overwhelmed and frightened and withdraw from your efforts.

For example, if you have a friend who isn't sure whether or not his son is an alcoholic, and you think the boy is an alcoholic, *even if you are absolutely right and correct in your opinion,* don't immediately tell him to call a rehab center to have his son checked in. Your plan is likely to backfire. Instead, help your friend think through it; face his denial, fears, and grief about his son's situation; and make the determination on his own. He is the one who will have to do the heavy lifting. He is the one who will need to own the decision. Be patient and allow him time and room to get from one stage to the next.

AS MUCH AS YOU ARE ABLE, BE PRESENT TO THE END OF THE PROCESS

People who are healing do better with continuous and stable relationships that stick with them and stand by them throughout the process. The changes they are going through can be very disruptive and disorienting. The more steady and reliable their relationships, the calmer and safer they feel inside and the better they are able to finish the path. It is hard to change healing relationships in the middle of the process. It is certainly not possible sometimes, with job, life, and schedule changes, but the more continuous things are, the better. Loving people invest in others for the long term. They keep their commitments and are there in fair and foul weather.

TAKING THE NEXT STEPS

Love heals. That is one of the primary things that loving people can be involved in. As we have said, make sure you are in the healing process, and get connected to those who are more experienced so they can train and mentor you. When you are helping another person, stay focused on them and the issue. Don't lose your reality. Know when to move out of pain. Help people to go past symptoms into causes. And be present with them. You will be amazed at how, over time, people you care about can transform.

Here are a few tips along the way:

- Put energy into the work of listening. Just as in the connecting chapter, much good can be done by accurately and empathetically understanding another person's experience. Check it out with them: "Do I understand that . . . ?" "Am I getting it that . . . ?"

- When you are not sure of what is going on, say it. Don't feel pressure to have all the answers. Healers know when they need to know more. This week, for example, in my office I told a counselee, "I'm just not getting it yet. Can I tell you where I am getting confused?"

- Make sure of your motives. Do not be a healer who is looking for a project! This should be about the needs of others, not your need to be needed.

- Ask your mentor or training group for feedback on your strengths and weaknesses. Do you need to work on empathy or confrontation or tying in the symptom to the issue or giving suggestions? Feedback can help a great deal.

My experience is that as people become more loving by becoming connected and truth-telling, they gradually become involved in healing. They kind of fall into the process. Then one day they look around and realize that.

It is not a mystery how this happens. This makes sense. When you seek and do what is best for someone, when you take initiative to have compassion, and when you risk honesty, people with pain are drawn to you because

LOVING PEOPLE HEAL BY SHOWING UP, FOCUSING ON WHAT IS BROKEN, AND BEING AN AGENT OF HEALING.

you have things they need to become whole. Loving people heal by showing up, focusing on what is broken, and being an agent of healing. You are making a difference, then, which can affect not only a person who is hurting today but also generations to come.

SIX

Letting Go: Accepting What Is

Joy and I have been friends for a long time, long enough to see her through the end of one marriage and the beginning of another. When Alan first began to tell her that he wasn't happy in the marriage and was thinking about leaving, it was an extremely painful and dark time for Joy. Before that, she had been aware that they didn't have a perfect connection. She figured things were basically OK; they were probably somewhere in the normal range of marriages, with the normal range of problems, and their relationship would most likely improve with time.

But Alan did not share her views. Within a few weeks he had moved out and rented an apartment. Of course, Joy was shocked and alarmed. What in the world had happened to them? Things had somehow speedily mutated from some distancing and arguments to the threat of the marriage being ended. So, because she loved Alan and wanted to save the relationship, Joy fought for their marriage. She did everything she could think of to make things better. She went to Alan and asked him to tell her what his unhappiness was about, and she listened without editing or rationalizing his feelings. She made sure she understood, when she perhaps had dismissed him or been defensive before. She apologized for and took ownership of the things he was right about. She made changes. She got into counseling and joined a growth group. She got spiritual direction from her pastor on how to make things better. She asked Alan to go to couples' counseling with her. She requested that he be open to marriage mentoring. She asked him to hold off on seeking a divorce until he had time to observe her changes and time for their counseling to take hold and show some benefits. She went the whole nine yards.

Unfortunately, Alan persisted in his desire to get out of the marriage and retained an attorney to begin divorce proceedings. And that was when Joy made her only serious error. She became frightened and therefore panicked. In her fear she became controlling with Alan. I think her reaction was because she had simply not been aware of how much he wanted out and how determined he was to leave. Her control manifested itself in more than one way, as is usually the case. She became emotional and demanding, calling often and going to his home to make him come back. She went to his friends and asked them to make him stay with her. She threatened him with legal hurt if he continued the proceedings. Alternately, she would also become compliant and self-abasing, apologizing for things that weren't bad and pleading with him to reconsider. She says now that she was not herself during this period, and she is glad it is over.

WHEN WE ALLOW REALITY TO WIN, WE CANNOT LOSE.

However, Alan was undeterred by Joy's attempts to control him. He ultimately divorced her. But while it was deeply disappointing for Joy, at the same time something new and good happened to her. Her emotions began to change inside. She began to feel calmer and more stable, even hopeful that she had a future without Alan. Of course, she was extremely sad and hurt, but there were other good things going on inside her as well.

In time, Joy moved on emotionally, personally, and spiritually. She finally met Dan, the man to whom she is now happily married. Things are much better. I talked to her about the process of the breakup and what it was like for her. She said, "I am glad that I did all the growth work I did when I was trying to keep the marriage together. It helped me not have any regrets today, and I think I would have some if I had just let the relationship go. At the same time, I am also glad that I did finally let Alan go. When I realized that nothing I could do was going to keep him with me, a light came on and I stopped the control and schemes. I gave up crossing the line and trying to make him love me and stay. And I think that not only helped me move on, but it also helps me with Dan today."

What Joy was basically saying was this: *when we allow reality to win, we cannot lose.* That is the nature and benefit of letting go and saying good-bye when it is time for that to happen.

THE NEGATIVE THAT IS A POSITIVE

Centuries ago, King Solomon understood the value and necessity of letting go and moving on in life. He wrote:

> For everything there is a season, a time for every activity under heaven.
> A time to be born and a time to die.
> A time to plant and a time to harvest.
> A time to kill and a time to heal.
> A time to tear down and a time to build up.
> A time to cry and a time to laugh.
> A time to grieve and a time to dance.
> A time to scatter stones and a time to gather stones.
> A time to embrace and a time to turn away.
> A time to search and a time to quit searching.
> A time to keep and a time to throw away.
> A time to tear and a time to mend.
> A time to be quiet and a time to speak.
> A time to love and a time to hate.
> A time for war and a time for peace.[1]

What does any of this have to do with love and being a loving person? A great deal. Sometimes love means knowing when it is time to let someone go or to let him do something he is going to do. When you accept reality and give up efforts to control someone's life or change who he is, you are being loving. Joy's situation is a good example.

Letting go is the ability to surrender and to allow what is real to exist. By letting go, I mean *giving up efforts to control, manipulate, or force someone to do something different.* It is accepting the truth. Sometimes the most loving thing to say to a person you care about is, "I understand what you're saying. I accept your freedom to do whatever it is you want." It's not as if the person doesn't have the freedom anyway. So you are not giving him anything he doesn't already possess. But it is important for your sake, and actually for the other person's sake, to validate that this is true and real.

The ability to let go is not one with which we are born. We all naturally want to control our relationships. In our minds, people are supposed to love us the way we need them to—and do it immediately. Usually, our impulse is to try to make someone or some situation bend toward what we want and need. When

> **LETTING GO IS THE ABILITY TO SURRENDER AND TO ALLOW WHAT IS REAL TO EXIST.**

our kids were younger, they would say, "I'll make you be nice to me!" But for adults, that is not how the laws of love and relationship work. Love cherishes and protects the freedom of both parties, as we discussed earlier. Control inhibits that freedom, so control works against being a loving person.

Consider this: if anyone could *make* someone love them, it would be God. He alone has the right and the power to do that if he wished. But he does not play that card with us, and he experiences pain and hurt for allowing us that freedom. Jesus' sad lament over people who were walking away from his love and salvation is a good description of his feelings about letting us go: "O Jerusalem, Jerusalem, the city that kills the prophets and stones God's messengers! How often I have wanted to gather your children together as a hen protects her chicks beneath her wings, but you wouldn't let me."[2]

God faces the reality of letting go. But in so doing, he makes it so that if we are ever to come to him and follow him, it will be of our own free will, not because he coerced or controlled us. He is not interested in a controlling sort of a relationship, for it is a poor model. It does not work. To the extent that we adopt God's viewpoint, we do better in life and love.

Letting go is a negative that is also a positive, not just for the other person but also for you. Most of the time, letting go and accepting reality hurts and is painful. How could it not be painful when you are experiencing someone you care about who is moving against you or away from you? But anytime you synchronize yourself with reality instead of trying to force reality to serve you, you cannot lose. And, as we will see, that pain is not permanent pain. The difficult feelings resolve themselves as we enter the process of learning to let go, and in time, though we sometimes don't believe it will happen, we begin to once again do life better and feel better.

SAY GOOD-BYE TO YOUR DEMAND . . .

A good way to get into the steps of letting go is to understand what you need to say good-bye to. As a loving person, you may need to say good-bye to some realities and attitudes that are not the best for you or the person you care about. Saying good-bye to things that will no longer exist is helpful for all of us. In fact, these are things which may be keeping you from the life you would like to have. Here are the basic ones to think about and deal with. These are what all of us need to let go of. In the following list, learn to say good-bye to any attempts to control or demands . . .

. . . FOR THE OTHER PERSON TO CHANGE

We would all like for those we love to be different in some way. It would make life and the connection easier, for example, for a person close to us to be kinder. To listen and attend better. To take more responsibility. To be less angry. To be less controlling. These are not bad things to ask for, and relationships do tend to improve when people make those shifts. The desire for positive change is a positive thing. However, you do not possess the right to demand or force people to change. Their choice and their freedom must always be respected and even protected. You must insist that they be in charge of their decisions and not attempt to change simply because they feel you are controlling or manipulating them. I assure you that you will not get the results you are asking for. In fact, it can make matters worse. They need to know that their choices are theirs alone. Then, and only then, can they take full responsibility for their actions. Otherwise you run the risk of either half-hearted compliance, which ultimately breaks down, or of them blaming you for their choices and you being resented for wanting them to change.

> LETTING GO IS A NEGATIVE THAT IS ALSO A POSITIVE, NOT JUST FOR THE OTHER PERSON BUT ALSO FOR YOU.

It helps to imagine the shoe being on the other foot. How would you feel if you were told, "You have to start paying more attention to me and being more caring. You must?" Those commands would not generate warmth or movement to change. Rather, as all of us, you would dig in your heels and think, *No, I don't have to.* Remember that attempts to control us make us feel like children. And the direction of every child is to move away from the parent. Do not force people in your life to push away even more than they have to. Give the same grace to them that you desire for yourself.

AS A LOVING PERSON, YOU MAY NEED TO SAY GOOD-BYE TO SOME REALITIES AND ATTITUDES THAT AREN'T THE BEST FOR YOU OR THE PERSON YOU CARE ABOUT.

So say good-bye to making someone choose to be more loving and different. You will no doubt encounter sad feelings, especially if you really care about the person, and if you are right about the matter, and if it would genuinely make things better for them and for the relationship. But you are better off with this approach.

That does not mean, however, that you are helpless and have no choices yourself. There are lots of things you can do. You cannot control the other person, but you can influence, talk, be vulnerable and humble, request, and negotiate. You just cannot demand. Also, you can protect yourself with requirements of how you are to be treated. Saying good-bye to making someone change is not creating yourself to be a doormat or a target for abuse. You can choose to remove yourself and get out of harm's way. And you can have requirements of what needs to happen for you to become accessible and close. That is, you may need to say, "For us to be intimate again, I can't have you yelling at me like that anymore. That is a requirement for me and for us from now on." In other words, you are saying, *You can be as selfish and mad as you would like. I want you to be free to. But at the same time, I will be using my freedom to be elsewhere when that happens.* That is what protecting choices for both of you is about. Love protects freedom.

. . . for Perfect Justice and Fairness

Life is not fair. We do not always reap what we sow, and neither do others. Innocent people get hurt, and bad guys get away with being bad guys. This is the way it has been ever since sin entered the universe.

Our natural response to this reality is to protest. It is not fair that other people will not forgive us, or that they take more than they give, or that they don't want us the way we want them. That is true. These things are not fair. And the protest is a good thing to experience. The protest helps us to identify hurtful things and people. It serves as an initial alert that something negative is going on so that we can understand and take action. It is a season of protest, and it helps us.

At the same time, *we also have a tendency to go beyond a season of protest to an identity of protest in our relationships.* That is, we sometimes adopt "It's not fair!" as a personal mantra. This attitude begins to surface no matter the situation: war, disease, relationships, and social issues. This works against people, because they become defined more by what they are against than by what they are for.

A person demanding perfect justice and fairness will always feel dissatisfied and will tend to be more preoccupied with getting their just treatment than they are with loving and being loved. It is often a major turning point in marital counseling when the couple begins to give up the demand for things to be equal between them. One person may be 80 percent of the financial problem, and the other 20 percent. One may be 90 per-

> THE DESIRE FOR POSITIVE CHANGE IS A POSITIVE THING. HOWEVER, YOU DO NOT POSSESS THE RIGHT TO DEMAND OR FORCE PEOPLE TO CHANGE.

cent of the connection problem, and the other 10 percent. This is not equal and fair. But it is reality. Work with the reality. Certainly try to change things, but give up the protest of withdrawing from the game because things do not balance out. In fact, one of the most loving things you can do in your relationship is to *expect to be let down.* Do not be surprised, shocked, or devastated when the other person's selfishness or irresponsibility emerges. It is there, and it is real. Expect it, and deal with it.

The ultimate solution is to go beyond justice and fairness and live in grace instead. Give more than you should. Do not give until it is fair and then stop. Do not stop at doing "your half." That is how people ruin relationships. Be a force for justice and fairness in your relationships, but do not require that the balance sheet be even for you to be a loving person.

> THE ULTIMATE SOLUTION IS TO GO BEYOND JUSTICE AND FAIRNESS, AND LIVE IN GRACE INSTEAD.

It is hard to imagine two people being close for many years and saying, "Our secret is that we don't love each other until the other person is fair with us." It doesn't work, especially in a universe created by a Designer who went far beyond fair—and aren't we glad he did? "For Christ also died for sins once for all, the just for the unjust, so that He might bring us to God."[3] Say good-bye to the demand for perfect fairness. Loving people give that up and live in grace.

. . . FOR ONE SPECIFIC PERSON TO MEET YOUR NEED

When you love someone, you carve out a place in your life and heart for that person, and you become invested in her presence in your own life. And the way love works, you ascribe some need to her and she is involved in helping meet your need. That is a good thing; it's how love works. For example, you may have been dating someone who is quite affirming and validating. She sees the good in you that others do not, and believes in you more than you do in yourself at times. You find yourself liking yourself better, accepting yourself, and becoming more confident.

Then the relationship ends for some reason, as most dating connections do. It can be very difficult, especially since she no longer is there to provide the affirmation and positive view of yourself. Often, a person will give up on feeling OK about himself, as the original source for that need is absent. He will become somewhat withdrawn or detached. Conversely, he may become argumentative with the other person, trying to insist that she reconsider the breakup so his need can be met again. This is a common tendency, demanding that a specific person meet our need. We are used to that person and their ways and manner. It is comfortable. That makes sense.

But this tendency to demand works against us. When we insist that no one else can be what that person was to us, we put ourselves in jeopardy of being alone and disconnected. While people matter a great deal, different individuals can provide the same needs in perhaps a different style. There are other affirming and validating people with whom we can meet and connect.

This demand is actually rooted in old developmental patterns. Young children are entirely dependent on their parents, so they have very few experiences with other nurturers and caretakers. Gradually, however, they learn to safely branch out and be loved by other relatives and friends. It is how they learn to interact with the world. But sometimes if a person has not finished that path, he will still maintain an old demand that "no one can love me like this other person did." This feeling is a signal that we need to move past the early stage, take some risks, and give other people a chance to connect with us.

Let me illustrate this point from a canine perspective. We have two Labrador retrievers, Heidi and Casey. Casey is a jumper, and until we figured out how she was scaling the lowest part of our backyard wall, we went through some interesting times losing her. On one occasion she was gone several hours when a woman who lived several blocks away called and said Casey was in her garage playing with her kids and eating their donuts. When we went to pick her up, Casey was glad to see us and jumped in the car to go home. But I think she would have been glad to stay with the other family. This is not a dog who will ever starve. She adopts herself to people quickly. I felt a little bad about it, like maybe she is not that attached to us. But the point is, Casey has not limited her desire for love and care to only one family.

If someone in your life chooses not to give you the care, affirmation, love, or help you need, do not starve and wait for them to come around. Get it elsewhere. Do not be held hostage by the situation. It is a freedom for you, and it is a loving thing that works all the way around.

. . . for Someone to Stay in a Relationship Who Wants to Leave It

The sad reality is often that, despite our best efforts to seek and do what is best for another person, relationships still end. People get divorced, dating relationships end, friendships break up, and family connections are severed. Some of these should happen, and some should not. Sometimes it is for the best, and sometimes it is harmful. Regardless, the ending of relationships is a reality. And it is one that, as a loving person, you need to surrender to and accept.

We need to let people go when they say they are leaving us. This is one of the most painful things anyone can experience. When you care about and love someone, being left can rip your heart out. But you will increase the damage if you try to demand or control that outcome. To force someone to stay with you when that person does not want to be there works against love and

LEARNING TO LET A PERSON GO, AND ENCOURAGING THAT PERSON TO MAKE A WHOLEHEARTED CHOICE, WHATEVER DIRECTION THAT IS, IS THE ONLY APPROACH THAT HAS ANY HOPE OF A GOOD OUTCOME.

growth. You will find yourself in the position of being with, but not with, someone. You will experience loneliness though it looks as if you are not alone. It is the shell of a relationship, but the heart is not present. That is not how relationships thrive in any sense of the word. Learning to let a person go, and encouraging that person to make a wholehearted choice, whatever direction that is, is the only approach that has any hope of a good outcome.

However, as in the situation above of wanting someone to change, you are not helpless either. This is not about being passive or fatalistic. As Joy did, fight for the relationship, do the work, put in the time. But ultimately, validate the other person's freedom. It is what God does every day: letting people have their will. I have seen many times that if there is hope that the relationship will stay intact, it is the letting go that gave the person pause to consider if that is what he really wanted. He was able to consider what that choice meant instead of being focused on not being controlled.

There is another important aspect here as well. *Sometimes the most loving thing for another is not your presence but your absence.* That is, there are times when what is truly best for that person is for you not to be in his or her life, for whatever reason.

For example, suppose you see that you are not the right person for a position in a business or an organization. Or if you are dating someone who is with you because of loyalty or history but there is someone else in her life who is truly a better fit for her than you are. If this is the case, you have to do what is most unnatural and counterintuitive and let go of the relationship for the other person's sake. Certainly this can be painful— and the more you care, the more painful it can be. But it actually stretches you to live out and fulfill the definition of what love is really all about. It is a sacrifice to let go when you seek the very best fit for that person.

> SOMETIMES THE MOST LOVING THING FOR ANOTHER IS NOT YOUR PRESENCE BUT YOUR ABSENCE.

THE ELEMENTS OF LETTING GO

Letting go is one of the hardest things about being a loving person, for it works against what you are doing. Generally, when you deeply care about a person, you want to move toward him or her. To let the person move in the opposite direction is difficult to bear. Fortunately, there are several elements of love that will really help you to let go in ways that work the best for yourself, the other person, and the situation.

FORGIVENESS

Technically the canceling of a debt, forgiveness is an essential part of letting someone go. When you forgive another person for wronging you, you are giving up your right to punish that person. And this can go a long way toward helping you to work through and resolve hurt feelings coming from giving up demands and control. This is because *forgiveness frees you from that person.*

This is important to understand, as the common perspective is that forgiveness frees the other person: he does not have to feel the consequences. But you are also freed when you cancel the debt. Forgiveness allows you to let go of your own needs and demands for the person to change, do right, apologize, or return. That is true freedom. Conversely, when we do not forgive, we stay entwined with that person, not being able to move on until the person

> FORGIVENESS ALLOWS YOU TO LET GO OF YOUR OWN NEEDS AND DEMANDS FOR THE PERSON TO CHANGE, DO RIGHT, APOLOGIZE, OR RETURN. THAT IS TRUE FREEDOM.

changes. In that sense, we stay dependent on another to the extent that we do not forgive. And it is a bad bet to be dependent on someone who is not doing the right thing.

GRIEF

The experience of sadness over a loss, grief helps loving people to also let go. When you grieve, you are doing some very helpful things for yourself. You are feeling what it feels like to accept reality. You are entering a process that is temporary and has an end to it rather than a permanent attempt to hang on to the person. And you are also valuing what you love and appreciate about the other person, which is a truly loving thing. You cannot grieve over someone you have no value for. So allow yourself to remember and be aware of what you desired, as well as what you did not like, in that person. As forgiveness does, grief lets you deal with reality and move on. This may mean staying in a relationship while at the same time feeling sad that it is not close to what you would have wanted. That helps you to be more successful in dealing well with what is actually there.

That is why the worst thing a friend can do with someone who must let another go is to devalue that person. It is a natural mistake to make, and the friend is generally trying to help, but it sets people back. You know how it goes: "Well, you are better off without her; she wasn't good enough for you anyway." That may be true. But statements like these negate and dismiss what the person loved: the other person's sense of humor, personality, shared experiences. So they never grieve the entire individual, just the toxic parts. Friends let friends say good-bye to the good and the bad.

ADAPTATION

Adaptation is the ability to adjust your life and ways to the realities in which you exist. Adaptive people change to meet the requirements of their circumstances. For example, a woman's husband shows no interest in a deeper connection with her. All her attempts to bring him closer to intimacy have met a dead end. He is happy with a more functional and distant relationship. Some adaptations she might make are to make sure she is connected regularly to her own team of loving and supportive people. She finds what common things she and her husband can do that at least provide contact, but she has her own activities that bring her joy. She is giving back and investing her gifts in service and helping others in some way. She lets him know that she is not going to be without a life if he does not want closeness, but she is open to it in the future if he decides he wants more of her.

FAITH

Trusting God for what you cannot and should not attempt to control will also help you let go of what you cannot keep. God knows that many times, the most loving thing is to release someone at some level. That is where the benefits of faith come in. Instead of being afraid of what will happen to you if the person does not change, or if there is no justice, or all the other things we become anxious about, ask him to provide and take care of matters. God knows what is best for you.

When we do not have faith, we run the risk of making an idol of the other person and investing too much in their actions and attitudes toward us. But when we put matters in his hands, we can love without controlling in our desperation: "Give all your worries and cares to God, for he cares about you."[4]

Faith was the final key for my friends George and Val, a couple whose son, Trent, rejected their values while still a teenager. For years, despite all their efforts of changing as parents, bringing in specialists and counselors, and sending him to treatment centers, he stayed ultra-rebellious and out of control. This has continued into his twenties. When kids become young adults, sometimes a pathological or psychological condition becomes a value and a lifestyle. Trent has had all sorts of opportunities to get help. He has consistently denied that there was any problem beyond parents who do not get it. He believed that his drug involvement, choices of friends, and work habits

> TRUSTING GOD FOR WHAT YOU CANNOT AND SHOULD NOT ATTEMPT TO CONTROL WILL ALSO HELP YOU LET GO OF WHAT YOU CANNOT KEEP.

were fine. Trent got himself in financial trouble repeatedly and looked to George and Val to bail him out. He himself now has a son whom he is not raising in the best way.

George and Val were brokenhearted and searching for many years. They had gone to any measures possible to help him. Then, finally, when Trent refused any sort of responsibility for his problems or his lifestyle, they put their trust in God and literally gave Trent to him. They told their son, "We love you, but we aren't going to nag or attempt to change you anymore. We will be glad to see you when we can. But there will be no drugs when we do. And we won't be giving you any more money." Trent was very angry at this and told them that they were judging him. He severely limited his contact with them. And worst of all, he made it harder for them to see their grandson. And they had to let that go.

The couple stayed with their faith-driven approach for several years. It tore them up, but they said good-bye to attempts to change or control Trent, even though it meant saying good-bye to Trent himself. But they knew that the best thing was to let go. And in time, on his own, Trent began to grow up. With no one to rescue him, he has become tired of being dependent and broke, and he has begun to seek help and counseling. The changes are slow, but they are real. And he now has more contact with his parents. George and Val paid the price of letting go and instead held on to God, who did not let them, nor Trent, go. Putting faith in God's care is investing your life and relationships in the right place.

TAKING THE NEXT STEPS

It is a temptation to skip this chapter, because it involves some sad realities. Do not make that mistake, however. The better you learn what to let go of, the more loving you will be. And ironically, the more full and fulfilled you will be. Remember to say good-bye to demands on others to change, to perfect justice, to thinking just one person can meet your needs, and to keeping someone who wants to leave. And the elements of forgiveness, grief, adaptation, and faith will help you do that.

Here are some tips to assist this process:

- Learn the art of saying what you would like in a relationship and arguing for it, but ultimately allow the other person to choose. That is the path to being a truly loving person.

- Become comfortable with tears. Tears are a part of life. I cry on a regular basis for all sorts of reasons: relationships, counselees, my own struggles, spiritual issues, movies, and so on. This is not by intent or decision at all. It is just that when there are sad things or losses in my life, I try not to stop the feelings and tears. Sadness is something you allow, not something that you do. And you must allow it. Do not run from sadness. It will end if you embrace it.

- When you let something or someone go, look for what will replace it. Don't live in a vacuum.

Fairy tales and Hollywood movies say that love is forever, at least the romantic type. But reality says that sometimes love is letting go—and that is truly letting go, without a backup. Loving people are individuals who, even though it hurts, are willing to give up demands and control in order to seek and do what is best for the other person. It is a pain that ultimately pays off, often with the other person, but without fail within your own life and growth. It is truly the negative that bears positive fruit!

SEVEN

Romancing: The Attraction Factor

Stephanie, a single friend of mine, was telling me some of her latest dating stories. She told me about a past relationship with a man named Spencer that had not ended well for her. Stephanie had been much more interested in Spencer than he was in her. He had not mistreated her in any way, and he actually was a good guy. He just didn't have reciprocal feelings for her. Ultimately, they moved on from each other. Stephanie was sad for a long time, since she had very strong feelings for Spencer, so the breakup was difficult for her.

Reflecting on that relationship, Stephanie said, "I think I had gotten through most of my feelings for Spencer as time passed. The other day, though, I ran into him at a party, and the weirdest thing happened. All of a sudden, I was back there in the old days again. I felt all the things I had originally felt for him, and the feelings were just as strong. He was still in my head."

I said, "That must have been tough."

She said, "It was, but that wasn't the important thing. What really got to me was what I was doing in my head with the feelings."

"What were you doing?"

She said, "I started thinking that if he wanted a relationship again, I would have gone for it that very second. I would have said, 'Yes, I'll get involved with you again.' Even if I knew for sure that it wouldn't work out. Even if I would be just as hurt again. I would have done it. It was insane. I could not believe how intense the emotions were."

Stephanie is an intelligent, thoughtful, professional person. But, as with all of us, she was vulnerable to the power and draw of romance, passion, and sexuality.

> ## IT IS ALMOST IMPOSSIBLE TO IGNORE THE PRESENCE OF ROMANCE IN OUR LIVES, ACTIVITIES, AND RELATIONSHIPS.

The good thing about Stephanie, however, is that she was able to observe romance from a more detached perspective. She did not assume her feelings were telling her the right things to do. At the same time, Stephanie's experience illustrates the reality of passion and the need we have to learn to deal with it in ways that we get the best from it for ourselves and for others.

So what is romance? Why is it so strong? Why do we experience it in the first place, and what is it to be used for? And ultimately, what does romance have to do with being a loving person?

THE ROMANCE=LOVE FORMULA

Romance, passion, and sex are on most people's radar screen. Romance is the stuff of films, TV, books, and magazines. It excites us, invites us, confuses us, hurts us, and makes us do things that don't seem sane—and sometimes aren't. It is almost impossible to ignore the presence of romance in our lives, activities, and relationships. Romantic love gets high marks in Scripture as well. The book in the Bible dedicated to romance begins with these words: "This is Solomon's song of songs, more wonderful than any other."[1] That is a serious endorsement. So romance is on God's radar screen as well as ours.

In fact, romance is such a significant concept in our culture that it is often considered equal to love itself. Think how many times you have been in the grocery store and seen statements like these on the magazines in the checkout line:

- "Actress X Finally Finds Love!"
- "Love Secrets of the Experts!"
- "How to Make Him Love You!"
- "Experiencing Love to the Fullest!"

- "Rate Your Love Life with This Quiz!"
- "Are You Really in Love?"

Interestingly, the next time you are in the checkout line, the same magazines will have very similarly worded titles and headings. This is as if to say that the month before, none of these ideas worked, so forget them and now do these; they will work for you. The full picture of love, however, is different in reality from the magazines. Romance is a wonderful aspect of love, but it is not as broad or as deep as love itself. Romance must fit into and serve love. Love can never serve romance. The best and most fulfilling romantic relationships are those that have this view and perspective, and they tend to be very happy with their love life. For they truly have a *love life*, not simply a romantic life.

> ROMANCE MUST FIT INTO AND SERVE LOVE. LOVE CAN NEVER SERVE ROMANCE.

UNCOVERING THE MYSTERY

You really can understand romance and passion to a greater degree than you might have realized. In fact, you should do this in order to experience and enjoy its benefits. I do not agree with the mind-set of romance being a mystery that cannot be understood or comprehended, for it should be experienced rather than analyzed. This sort of perspective advises us to simply feel romantic feelings, and enjoy them while they last. In this thinking, people often end up without a sense of control or choice about romance. Sometimes romance even controls them, which can be a life problem.

But the reality is that there actually is a lot you can know and comprehend what romance truly is, and this will help you in your relationships. The essence of romance has been thought about, observed, broken down, researched, and explored by many perceptive people.

Having said that, however, there certainly is, and always will be, a certain mystery to romance, passion, and sexuality, which makes it all the more attractive to us. As a proverb says, "There are three things that are too amazing for me, four that I do not understand: the way of an eagle in the sky, the way of a snake on a rock, the way of a ship on the high seas, and the way of a man with a maiden."[2] Take, for example, those instances in which two strangers make eye contact, and for some unknown reason, there is chemistry on both sides that can be intense and strong. That is actual and real, and the experience should not be ignored. So we should enjoy and appreciate the mystery aspect. But also, let's learn about the DNA part so that you can have the best of romance that you can. As with every other aspect of being a loving person, romance is something you can have some control over.

> **AS WITH EVERY OTHER ASPECT OF BEING A LOVING PERSON, ROMANCE IS SOMETHING YOU CAN HAVE SOME CONTROL OVER.**

Here is a simple definition: *Romance is a temporary idealization of the other person that increases passionate and sexual attraction.* When we idealize the other person, we see that person, for the moment, as perfect and good, with no faults or blemishes. In romantic settings, the lover is initially only aware of the positive qualities of the beloved: his smile, face, quirks, tenderness, emotionality, strength, values, and so on. It can be a very long list. In fact, sometimes we see qualities in the other person that are not there because we want and desire for those qualities to be there. This does not mean you are in denial about reality or are making things up when you feel romantic. If someone asked you at that moment, "Does he have any flaws?" you would most likely say, "Of course he does." Romance is not a break from reality as much as a focus and a concentration on the good parts. In a technical sense, it is part of connection. It is a special and unique type of attachment between two people, with its own characteristics.

Because it focuses on positive aspects, romance is a positive feeling. It is pleasant, is energizing, and makes us feel alive and vibrant. So it reinforces itself. We have romantic feelings for someone, so we talk to that person. If things go well, the romance increases, which increases the contact with the person and so forth. It is powerful and intense.

Romance has purposes, as everything designed by God does. It brings men and women together to unite in love and marriage. It is pleasurable in and of itself. And it has a particularly important function in the early stages of relationships. *Romance helps us to establish a bond and attachment that hopefully will be strong enough to handle and deal with the negatives and problems of relationships.* The idealization provides a foundation to be able to then live with reality. Romance, then, is a sort of bridge in a relationship, so that when conflicts and issues arise, the two people have a good history of connection, positive experiences, and care.

HOW DOES ROMANCE FIT INTO LOVE?

How does passion fit into our overall definition of love in this book, which is "seeking and doing the best for another"? *Romance is ultimately, and at its highest level, the reward of love.* It is a payoff, a fruit, a result. The effort and self-sacrifice of love has a benefit for couples, and that is the experience itself, which increases the pleasure of the relationship.

I have seen this happen often. Two people who have lost romance will learn instead how to love each other—that is, to seek and do what is best for their mate: they will begin to connect, tell the truth, and help each other heal. And during this process, romance will emerge between them, often better than it was before. This is the result of the work of love.

Romance serves us better as a benefit than it does as a goal in life. If our primary focus is to find romance, and we neglect love, we are at risk to have a series of intense, temporary, and ultimately unsatisfying relationships.

While romance is great and especially exciting at the beginning of a relationship, this stage of love is actually somewhat overrated. How hard is it to be strongly attracted to someone you do not really know? It requires no effort at all. You can fill in the blanks of what you do not know and make an ordinary person into a movie star in your mind. People do that all the time. Passion is far more valuable as time goes on in the relationship. The best, strongest, most satisfying, and deepest romance is that between two people who know each other's secrets, flaws, hurts, and weaknesses. And at

> ROMANCE IS ULTIMATELY, AND AT ITS HIGHEST LEVEL, THE REWARD OF LOVE.

the same time, they have the capacity to, for a temporary period of time, focus on the good and become more attracted to the person.

Why won't romantic love create a loved person out of an unloved one? For several reasons. First, romantic love has a basis in attractiveness. That is, we feel romantic toward someone because that person has qualities and traits to which we are drawn. In other words, there is a condition involved. If you do not find the person attractive, you may not feel romantic toward him.

Now put yourself on the receiving end of this equation. Someone shows romantic interest in you and pursues you. They tell you how desirable you are and all the qualities they admire in you: your looks, your smile, your sense of humor. That is well and good, but suppose for some reason that you lost some of those attractive qualities, either temporarily or permanently. What happens to the love you are receiving then? That is not a very secure position to be in. The love you are receiving is based on traits that may not exist.

YOU ARE BETTING ON THE WRONG HORSE WHEN YOU ATTEMPT TO MAKE ROMANTIC LOVE THE WAY TO DEAL WITH THE UNLOVED STATE.

This is often what happens when people get too romantic too quickly. They are "in love with being in love," and they shortcut getting to know someone's character and true self. Then, when looks start to go, or the sense of humor gets stale, the relationship breaks up. This can be a devastating experience. You are betting on the wrong horse when you attempt to make romantic love the way to deal with the unloved state.

Also, romantic love has no place for the dark side of life. That is, the idealization aspect of romance does not know what to do with weaknesses, fights, conflicts, selfishness, brokenness, sins, and the like. In fact, most people have had the experience of their romantic feelings diminishing when these problems arise. Then, when they solve the problems, the romance returns. Romance works best when it fits into the larger context of what authentic love produces.

THE ROMANCE ADDICTION

Viewing romance as equal to love is part of what creates romance addicts. These people live for romance and feel alive only when they are in love. They love the intensity of the passion, but it is based on some idealization either of the person or of the entire process. Then, when reality comes in the form of a conflict or weakness, they feel disappointed and search for the next romance. It is a tough existence, having serial romances and watching the years pass by with no direction, purpose, or progress in finding deep and lasting love.

I worked with a woman, Bridget, who had this tendency. She truly wanted to settle down and marry, but she continued a pattern of intense, emotional, passionate connections that never went anywhere. Her relationships were centered on dinners and trips, gifts and emotions. Yet they also involved heartbreak, drama, and alienation. Bridget had experienced some real dating nightmares. Worst, however, was that her friends were getting married and she was still dating at an age she thought by which she would be married. This fueled even more intense relationships in the search, and the cycle continued.

As Bridget and I began working together, I told her, "You have some really good friends, and you don't appreciate them. Until you do, you will stay in this pattern that is not working for you."

She was a little annoyed. "That is not true. I appreciate my friends very much. They support me during these bad times. I don't know what I would do without them."

"I agree with part of that," I said. "You do allow them to support you. But you don't appreciate what they could be bringing to you. I think you use them to talk about the men in your life. These friends comfort you, encourage you, give you advice, and put you back together when you are having a bad time with a man. But it's not about you and them. It's about them helping you with the goal of a man."

Bridget was quiet for a bit. Then she said, "I don't like to hear this, but you may be right. That is mostly what we talk about."

I said, "The problem is, you need to be getting from them what you think you should get from a man. Things like acceptance, understanding of who you are, and empathy for your feelings. I think you look over their heads and long for romantic love to fill you, when what you need to fill you is right in front of you. These boyfriends aren't your family. Some of them are OK, but they are still transitory. That's what I mean by truly appreciating your friends. They are your family, and you need to act like they are your family."

Bridget got it. And she began making the shift. She started really investing in her friends' lives, hopes, and dreams and sharing the other parts of her life with them, such as her career hopes, her weaknesses, and her childhood experiences. She got very close to several of these women and connected at a deep level with them.

> THE BEST MARRIAGES ARE THOSE IN WHICH THE COUPLE HAS SEVERAL OTHER FRIENDSHIPS WHO ARE SAFE, LOVING, AND "FOR" THE MARRIAGE.

Finally, she reported to me, "Something is different inside. I still do want to be married, no question about it. But that desire doesn't have the intensity it used to. My life with my friends is really good. I am OK, married or single."

On top of that, Bridget's quality of dating life also improved. Instead of finding guys who were romance and sex addicts themselves, she began going out with men who had character, lived healthy lives, and were interesting people. Her ability to pick and discern went up markedly. Romance is designed for one relationship at a time, and you need to receive love from several sources. Though the dating years may involve seeing several people, the final goal of romantic love is filtering things down to one person you want to love and hopefully marry. And that is it. Marriage involves one person making a heart-and-soul complete connection to another person. And that is very good.

But marriage, even a great one, is not enough. You need friends and close connections with whom you have no sexual or romantic ties. These people can give you what you need to receive, especially during tough times in the marriage. The best marriages are those in which the couple has several other friendships who are safe, loving, and "for" the marriage. These marriages have support resources that help and sustain them.

The marriages that suffer are those in which one spouse thinks his mate's love is all he needs. The problem here is that his mate has symbolically taken the role of his parent. She is the giver of life and love to him. And there is an imbalance that is bad for both individuals and their connection. So if you hope to date, or are dating, or are married, that is a good thing. It is to be sought after and developed. But appreciate the relationship for what it is, and do not confuse it for the other aspects of love that you need at the truly deepest level.

CREATING ROMANCE

Here are some principles for creating, developing, and experiencing the kind of romance, passion, and sexuality that actually does last, not the kind that you could read about next month at the checkout line.

DO THE UNDONE ASPECTS OF LOVE IN YOUR RELATIONSHIP

Romantic breakdowns almost always have relational breakdowns underlying them. When couples lose passion, it can be that they just have been pre-occupied or are taking each other for granted. More often than not, however, there is some hurt, misunderstanding, or problem underneath. So dig it up and deal with it. Identify where you and your mate are disconnected emotionally. Is there detachment or withdrawal? Irresponsibility? Control? Lack of respect? Blame? Denial? Unforgiveness? These matters need to be on the table and dealt with.

One of the worst things a couple can do is to try to feel more romantic while deeper issues are unresolved. It just doesn't work and, in fact, prohibits romance. You may as well go to the gym, work out for an hour, then skip the shower and put some cologne on, hoping to seem fresh and clean to the world. The world knows the truth, and so will you. Instead, "take the shower" of doing the work between you two.

ONE OF THE WORST THINGS A COUPLE CAN DO IS TO TRY TO FEEL MORE ROMANTIC WHILE DEEPER ISSUES ARE UNRESOLVED.

LOVE AND BE LOVED BY OTHERS BESIDES YOURSELVES

You need other sources of love for your relationship in order to develop passion. Otherwise, one person in the relationship will stifle the other. In a dating or marriage relationship, it helps to have three sets of close, vulnerable friendships: yours, mine, and ours. Ideally, the "ours" is the larger number. But metaphorically speaking, when you have healthy friendships in addition to your romantic relationship, you are infusing the immune system with healthy vitamins and minerals. Romance works better when you have this balance.

REQUIRE THAT BOTH OF YOU HAVE CHOICES AND FREEDOM

The heat of romance and sexuality intensifies when it is between two separate, choosing, free individuals. Your separateness helps you both feel and experience the reality that you are two distinct individuals. It creates space in the connection, and that allows passion. It is similar to when you have been apart from each other for several days, or even after an argument that you had.

Think about it: love, by definition, requires two people—the lover and the "lovee." The more evident it is that you are two separate people, the more the romance can grow. But the less you require choice and freedom, the more things get muddy and fuzzy between you two—as if you are not sure if there is one person or two. If the relationship tends toward the "we are one" end, people are vulnerable to a loss of passion. There just is no room for things to heat up.

INSIST ON CONNECTION BEFORE AND DURING ROMANCE AND SEX

Sex is, in its best sense, a product of intimacy, not an avenue for it. That is why I believe that sex should be reserved for the full-life commitment of marriage. Only the marital bond can bring sexuality to its highest, most vulnerable and most satisfying expression. Anything less tends to lead to heartbreak and a decline in the relationship. And since the most vulnerable and exposed thing you can do in a relationship is to be naked and unashamed, both of you need to know you are safe, connected, and cherished. Otherwise, sex can fragment and divide your relationship, and even your own heart inside you.

Connecting, as we described in Chapter 3, should generally be a prerequisite for sex to be truly relational and romantic. Tell your spouse, "I have to talk and connect to feel close enough to be romantic. I want to feel desire, but it's difficult when we are distant, and then you just want to be sexual." Of course there are exceptions to this. Certainly, spontaneous and fun sexuality is a great part of marriage. But pay attention to the relationship temperature as the norm.

The same is true during sex and romance. Be aware of, and express, your loving and connecting feelings toward the other person during the process. As you feel your emotions of care, along with your physical sensations, you are bringing body and soul together. You and your spouse are not divided inside, and you are not divided in your relationship.

> SEX IS, IN ITS BEST SENSE, A PRODUCT OF INTIMACY, NOT AN AVENUE FOR IT.

PAY ATTENTION TO THE EXPERIENCES OF THE BOTH OF YOU

Romance is limited when you focus only on your own feelings, sensations, and experiences. It is less relational then, and it is ultimately less pleasurable. The best sex and romance happen when you also pay attention to how the other person is doing. It can be extremely pleasurable to enjoy the pleasure the other person is having because of you, as well as your own. This is a balancing act between several experiences: your emotional love and attraction to the other; your physical sensations; and the other's experience. This sort of intentional flow of the focus of attention can heighten everything between you two.

THE SWORD CUTS BOTH WAYS

The experience of passion, like anything else intense and emotional, can be a two-edged sword. It can be helpful and not so helpful; it can add excitement and closeness to your life, and it can alienate and harm you and others—just ask any romance addict about the damage they have undergone.

So, as a loving person, it is important to learn when romance is OK and when it is not. Remember that love, in its basic definition, should be constant and unending: seeking and doing the best for someone is a value and stance, a way of life. But sometimes it can be the wrong time to connect, such as when you need to confront a bad behavior. Or sometimes you need to not confront because you might be too upset and risk doing it wrong.

In the same vein, there are times when romance should be withheld.

SOMETIMES THE MOST LOVING THING YOU CAN DO IS TO NOT BE ROMANTIC.

These are those occasions and situations in which the purposes of love are best furthered by *not* being, expressing, or entering into a romantic context. It may sound strange, but it is true: *sometimes the most loving thing you can do is to not be romantic.* You could be saving a relationship or a life by this attitude. Though it seems counterintuitive, we need to understand this, for it is very important in how well and completely we love others. Here are some times when it might be best to hold off from passion, romance, or sexuality.

WHEN IT SUBSTITUTES FOR CLOSENESS

As I discussed above, connection is essential before and during romance and sex. Sometimes one person may attempt to shortcut the process of connecting by getting sexual, saying romantic things, getting physical, and so forth before a genuine connection has taken place. Don't think that after sex that person will then open up and be vulnerable and empathetic. It just does not happen that way. So be honest and hold your ground: "I want to give myself to you, but not when you're only giving me part of yourself."

WHEN THERE IS A SERIOUS PROBLEM THAT IS BEING AVOIDED

Suppose your lover is an alcoholic, or an addict, or has a serious bipolar disorder that he is in denial of. Sometimes couples will try to be romantic, thinking that the positive feelings will help the person become safe enough to be motivated to change. Unfortunately, the opposite is generally true. Sex and romance instead act as an anesthetic to the discomfort the person is feeling, which should be driving him to get help or change. He feels temporarily better, loved, and comfortable, so he can go a little longer without dealing with the problem.

WHEN THERE IS HARMFUL TREATMENT

Sex and love should be based on values, compassion, and respect. They should have no place with hurtfulness, control, belittlement, or abuse. If one person is being injurious, everything should stop until there has been a frank discussion on what is OK and what is not OK in the relationship, and until there has been change. Do not send the message that the other person can treat you any way he feels like, and that there are no consequences to that. The consequence of hurtfulness should be that people withdraw from us and confront us. Be part of the solution, not the problem.

This does not mean, however, that you should demand that the other person be flawless before you will become romantic or sexual. It is OK for imperfect people to have sex and romance! Do not insist on something you cannot do yourself. Rather, set and insist on reasonable standards of treatment that apply to both of you. I get troubled when, on occasion, a man comes to me and says that in the name of boundaries, his wife set unrealistic demands on him and withdrew from him. If what he said is true, he is not being treated right; he is being judged or controlled.

> IT IS OK FOR IMPERFECT PEOPLE TO HAVE SEX AND ROMANCE!

For example, I was troubled when a man told me that because he was irritated with his wife, not yelling or abusive, she told him he was being controlling and withdrew from the relationship. If this is truly what happened, the consequence did not fit the offense. Harmful treatment causes harm. Spouses cannot be perfect, but their imperfections do not always cause injury.

WHEN SOMEONE WOULD BE INJURED

Since romance and sex involve so much vulnerability, sometimes a person with a wound may need to refrain from sexuality for some period of time. For example, a wife who is dealing with childhood sexual abuse might risk further harm if she has sex because of her fragility. If this is the case, she should seek help from an expert, and the couple should consult with that person about the best way to approach this. In most cases, with patience, love, and hard work, the couple can at some point resume sexual relations when the appropriate healing has taken place.

WHEN ROMANTIC FEELINGS ARE OUT OF DEFICIT, NOT TRUE LOVE

Look at what is driving your romantic feelings. In a perfect world, the idealization should be based on love, appreciation for the person's character, shared history and values, celebration, and so forth. But romantic feelings can spring from other unhealthy sources. For example, neediness, emptiness, dependency, attempts to make someone love us, repetition of childhood patterns, helplessness, anger, and self-absorption can also create romantic feelings that are every bit as strong and passionate.

Psychologists refer to this as *sexualization*—that is, making something sexual that really isn't. The man who wants sex because he's had a failure at work is sexualizing his need to feel sad and receive empathy from his wife, because it is easier and seems safer. The woman who becomes sexual when she wants her husband to stop being a flirt is sexualizing her fear of confronting and resolving the issue with him. When you identify these sources, deal with them instead of getting lost in a romance that will turn on you both.

FOR SPIRITUAL PURPOSES

One of the practices and disciplines of the faith is that of temporarily abstaining from sexuality for spiritual growth reasons. The principle involved is to establish self-control over our physical selves in order to focus on the spiritual parts: "Do not deprive each other of sexual relations, unless you both agree to refrain from sexual intimacy for a limited time so you can give yourselves more completely to prayer. Afterward, you should come together again so that Satan won't be able to tempt you because of your lack of self-control."[3] Much like periodic fasting, going on silent retreats, and the like, temporary abstention keeps us mindful of the transcendent realities of life.

TAKING THE NEXT STEPS

Viva passion, romance, and sex! And remember that the best way to experience these gifts is to understand that they are the fruit of love not the cause of it (sorry, guys). Make sure that you are working on growth, vulnerability, connection, and freedom with each other. And be prepared to not engage in sex and passion if something toxic is going on that is being avoided. Deal with it and then get on with the closeness and love you desire.

Here are some tips that can help:

- Normalize talks about passion, romance, and sex. Couples who talk about everything except these matters do not get the full experience. Make sexual and romantic discussions something you do and not just in passionate contexts but at the kitchen table over coffee or while taking a walk. You will be surprisd how free it will make you as a couple.

- Do not ignore the Hollywood trappings. They do have value: candles, lighting, bubble baths, different settings, and so on. They can enhance the experience. Just keep them the servant, not the master.

- Talk about your desires and lack of desires. Sometimes couples will find they are very different in what they want, but the connection helps them work out suitable compromises.

- Giving means giving as the other person wants it, not as you think the person does. Do not make this common mistake. The stereotype is that the wife thinks the man wants a back rub, and he thinks she wants sex. Keep in mind what the other person is feeling and desiring.

- Get another couple to talk to, mentor you, and help. These are matters that everyone deals with, and safe people can help you.

Discover the love that lies underneath the passion. Get to the character and the person first. If things are going the right way, you will experience more fulfilling, intense, and connected romance the way God designed it.

PART 3

Becoming a Loving Person

EIGHT

Putting It All Together

Since you have made it this far in reading this book, you are likely a person who is genuinely concerned about caring about others. Otherwise it wouldn't make sense that you would spend this much time on this kind of material. As I said earlier, this is not a self-help book, because it's ultimately not about self. It is, rather, about being the kind of self who loves well and thoroughly. It is for people who desire to extend themselves beyond their normal capacities. Who want to be able to get inside the hearts and lives of others and do good. Who want to give and make a difference. It means that you want to provide for others what they may not have been able to provide for themselves. And it means that you want to give back what has been given to you. And that is one of the highest motives anyone can have.

The reality is, love does change things, more than any one force in the universe. In a very fundamental and powerful way, it is loving people who, all the way through the pages of history, have made the most meaningful differences for good in the world. Loving people give hope to those who are hopeless. They provide growth for those who want to be better people. They give forgiveness to those under the lash of guilt and shame. They bring light to the lonely. They give a path to those who are confused and lost. They give of

> THE REALITY IS,
> LOVE DOES
> CHANGE THINGS,
> MORE THAN
> ANY ONE FORCE
> IN THE UNIVERSE.

themselves to the poor and needy. They take care of their families. They cause movements in the church. They develop leaders in areas that leadership is sorely needed.

All this effort and all this fruit bearing comes from that initial step to do what is best for others. When you decide to become the loving person you were designed to be, you are empowered by God himself to help not only your life and those close to you but help many people in a ripple effect whom you might never meet. The design for being loving and bearing fruit was created and built within you a long time ago. In Jesus' words, "You didn't choose me. I chose you. I appointed you to go and produce lasting fruit."[1]

WHERE DO YOU GO FROM HERE?

At this point, I would like to help you put it all together. What are the next steps for becoming the loving person you would like to be? Here are some ways to begin the journey.

ASSEMBLE YOUR TEAM

You cannot develop or grow your capacity to love in a vacuum. If there is anything that love teaches us, it is that we shouldn't be alone, especially in our own efforts to grow and change. So you need some help, a team. It is not just you, nor even just you and God. It is always you, God, and others who care. Think of, identify, and select a few people who seem to have a healthy perspective and experience of love and relationships. Let them know that you want to grow in this area of life. They can be part of the experience for you. Or they can simply be supporting your efforts and your path. The important thing is that you need others to walk the path with you.

IDENTIFY THE AREA OF NEED

It will help you to get specific about which aspects of love you feel the most need for and the most interest in, ranging from connecting to truth-telling, healing, letting go, and romance. I suggest that you look over your own life and think about which of these areas emerge most prominently. For example, do you find that it is hard to be direct with others? Or do you allow toxic people and situations to take things further than you really wish? In this way, you can best take action first on the area that relates to where you live today and which matters most. Once you have done that, begin to work on applying the principles in that chapter, using your team for support and grace.

DECIDE ON YOUR TIME INVESTMENT

You may need to carve out time on your schedule to work on these ideas and suggestions. It will take some time and effort away from other things you do, but the payoff is worth it. If you are already in some sort of growth context, such as a small group, you may not need to net out more time to do this. You already have the time allotted for growth, and you can use it for this material and content. The growth process is designed to work easily in that framework. Regardless, as you have probably seen, becoming more loving is simply not just an experience but a dedication of your values, behavior, and heart. So make sure you are spending the time you need for this.

NORMALIZE STRUGGLE AND OBSTACLES

Be aware that there are forces within and without that will emerge into the picture as you become more loving. This is only to be expected and should not surprise or discourage you. We all have our own fears and inertia. Love is risky and gets us out of our comfort zone. So be prepared for feelings of negativity or doubt.

Most likely, you'll also find that some people in your life will resist your changes. This may seem strange. Why would anyone not want you to care? Well, there are some good reasons. If you begin asking for love yourself, you may challenge another's idea of you as the strong one to depend on. If you connect, you may scare another who is more comfortable with distance. If you tell the truth,

> IF THERE IS ANYTHING THAT LOVE TEACHES US, IT IS THAT WE SHOULDN'T BE ALONE, ESPECIALLY IN OUR OWN EFFORTS TO GROW AND CHANGE.

> BECOMING MORE
> LOVING IS SIMPLY
> NOT JUST AN
> EXPERIENCE BUT
> A DEDICATION
> OF YOUR VALUES,
> BEHAVIOR, AND HEART.

you can certainly rock the boat. If you become more healing, you may incur jealousy or the negative feelings people experience when they begin to open up. If you let go, you may anger someone who wants you to maintain control. And if you move into romance, you may threaten someone who would like to have no feelings at all. The point is, love does shake things up; therefore be ready. But it is always worth the effort.

LOSE YOURSELF IN THE PROCESS

Since love has a lot to do with values and experiences, I think it is best to not be excessively behavioral and time-based in your growth. While becoming loving does have a structure and an order, as outlined in the chapters, you still need to have room for reflection, space, exploration, thoughts, feelings, conversations, and prayer. In other words, get involved in the experience.

That is what I mean by "lose yourself." I do not mean lose your identity or sense of self here. Rather, I am referring to the ability to get so engaged and caught up in love that you stop being overly concerned about the passage of time. This helps you to learn, grow, and experience what you need to. That is just the nature of the journey.

Can you imagine a honeymooning couple saying, "It's Monday, so let's connect for a couple of hours. What shall we talk about?" That wouldn't occur to them. Instead, they'd be so busy connecting and being in the moment with each other that they would not be aware of the passage of time. In fact, the more aware they are of time, the worse sign that is for their relationship. In the same way, get involved in the activities and the experiences of love. This, in my mind, is a little like being in the state of eternity, the way we were designed originally. It is where God lives, and it is all about being here, present and engaged.

MEASURE AND EVALUATE YOUR PROGRESS AND GROWTH

Losing yourself, however, is not something that is continuous; it occurs at various times and periods. Equally important is the task of measuring how

you are doing. Look at the qualities and issues of
your relationships, and how you respond and
react to them. Check with your team how you are
doing. You will be able to see if you are becoming
more of the person you want to be by the nature
of the connections you are working with, and
being supported by.

> YOU CANNOT
> OVERESTIMATE THE
> VALUE GOD PLACES
> ON LOVE.

KEEP IN MIND THE BIG PICTURE OF GROWTH

Remember that love serves your growth in all the significant areas of our days:
spiritual, personal, emotional, and relational. As you grow, change, practice
humility, own your baggage and issues, invest your time and talents, and stay
in relationships, love will continue to develop in you. God is actively on your
side, and he is your biggest support and resource. You cannot overestimate the
value God places on love. It is greater than faith and greater than hope.[2]

TAKING THE NEXT STEPS

At this point, I hope that you feel encouraged and prepared to become the loving person you were designed to be. True love, defined as "seeking and doing
the best for another," is an integral part of a life as it should be lived. Its benefits make all parts of our lives work in better and richer ways. This sort of love
brings people together in deeper and more meaningful ways; it is the foundation of all growth and change; and it is the missing ingredient of all great
romance. It is a value, a stance, and a way of life. And when we approach relationships in that way, we benefit from this definition. You cannot go wrong
here—no matter how the other person responds or does not respond. It is your
willingness to do the love, and love the right way, that truly matters.

A FINAL THOUGHT

Remember how this book began:

"I love you."

These three words can change your life.

They can, and they have, for ages. They are powerful and can transform any relationship and any person. Hopefully, however, now you will know just what you mean when you say those three words to another person. And much more importantly, you will now know what to do as well. That is the essence of being a loving person.

Love is the center of our being, and our minds, bodies, actions, and lives should reflect how we should live, choose, and connect. And that is because love is at the center of who God is and how he operates, for he is Love.[1] The debt we have to love, and the command to love each other, is so central that the Bible calls it "the royal law"—that is, the king of all laws. "Yes indeed, it is good when you obey *the royal law* as found in the Scriptures: *'Love your neighbor as yourself.'*"[2]

> **"I LOVE YOU."**

I hope you feel permission to be yourself as you begin and continue the process of being a loving person. The steps I have outlined in this book fit any life, personality, and situation. You do not have to be a professional therapist, counselor, or minister. Nor do you need to be married, be dating, or have kids. The world can use more people who are willing to grow in love no matter what their current life circumstances.

There may be lots of people around you who fit the descriptions here. Or

THE WORLD,
YOUR COMMUNITY,
YOUR FAMILY,
AND YOUR FRIENDS
NEED LOVING
PEOPLE LIKE YOU.

perhaps you have been able to identify with people who carry the weight of one particular aspect very well and who you want to learn from. People who can connect, tell the truth, heal, let go, and enter into romance can also help you grow, if those are the areas you want to grow in. These are individuals who can be of great value to you in putting all this together.

The world, your community, your family, and your friends need loving people like you so that they, too, may grow, change, find God, and ultimately become loving people who will continue the path. Your extension of yourself into the lives and hearts of others is one of the most deeply valuable and spiritual things any of us can do. I wish you well on that task.

God bless you,
Dr. John Townsend
Newport Beach, California

NOTES

Chapter 1—Learning to Love

1. 1 Corinthians 13:1
2. C. S. Lewis, *The Four Loves* (New York: Harcourt & Brace, 1988), 121.
3. John 13:34

Chapter 2—The Nature of Love

1. R. Laird Harris, Gleason L. Archer, and Bruce K. Waltke, *Theological Wordbook of the Old Testament* (Chicago: Moody, 1980), 14.
2. Deuteronomy 4:37
3. Genesis 22:2
4. Proverbs 20:13
5. Proverbs 5:19
6. Colin Brown, ed. *The New International Dictionary of New Testament Theology*, vol. 2 (Grand Rapids: Zondervan, 1986), 547–51.
7. Hebrews 13:1; emphasis added
8. Brown, ed. *The New International Dictionary of New Testament Theology*, 538–47.
9. John 15:12; emphasis added
10. John 3:16
11. Mark 12:30
12. Matthew 22:39
13. Helen Fisher, *Why We Love* (New York: Henry Holt, 2004).
14. Eric Jaffe, "Mirror Neurons: How We Reflect on Behavior" *Psychological Science* 20, no. 5 (May 2007), available at http://www.psychologicalscience.org.

15. Dorret I. Boomsma, John T. Cacioppo, P. Eline Slagboom, and Danielle Posthuma, "Genetic Linkage and Association Analysis for Loneliness in Dutch Twin and Sibling Pairs Points to a Region on Chromosome 12q 23-24." *Behavior Genetics* 36, no. 1 (January 2006).

16. M. Mikulincer and P. R. Shaver, *Attachment in Adulthood: Structure, Dynamics and Change* (New York: Guilford, 2007).

17. Louise C. Hawkley and John T. Cacioppo, "Aging and Loneliness: Downhill Quickly?" *Current Directions in Psychological Science* 16, no 4 (August 2007): 187–91.

18. Deuteronomy 4:40; emphasis added

19. Matthew 5:43–48

20. 1 Peter 3:18 NIV

21. Proverbs 6:16–19

22. Isaiah 61:8

23. Zechariah 8:17

24. Malachi 2:16

25. Romans 12:9

26. John Townsend, *Who's Pushing Your Buttons* (Nashville: Thomas Nelson Publishers, 2004).

Chapter 3—Connecting: Bridging the Gap

1. 2 Corinthians 6:11–13

2. John 15:5–7

3. Acts 20:35

4. Acts 20:32

5. Psalm 56:8

6. James 4:2 NIV

7. Matthew 10:8

8. Ephesians 3:17 NASB

9. Joel 2:25 NIV

10. 2 Corinthians 1:4 NIV

11. 2 Corinthians 13:14 NIV

12. Genesis 2:18

13. Ecclesiastes 4:10

14. Matthew 26:38 NASB
15. 2 Corinthians 7:6
16. 1 Peter 4:10 NASB
17. Psalm 68:6
18. Hebrews 2:18
19. Proverbs 20:5 NIV

Chapter 4—Truth-Telling: Solving Problems

1. Psalm 85:10
2. Romans 7:19, 24–25
3. My book *Hiding from Love* (Grand Rapids: Zondervan, 1996) and my book with Henry Cloud, *It's Not My Fault* (Nashville: Thomas Nelson, 2007), both deal with this issue.
4. My book *Who's Pushing Your Buttons?* (Nashville: Nelson, 2004), provides steps for dealing with difficult people who do not take ownership of their effect on others.
5. My book with Henry Cloud, *How to Have That Difficult Conversation You've Been Avoiding* (Grand Rapids: Zondervan, 2006) provides step-by-step instructions on how to confront effectively.
6. Matthew 7:5

Chapter 5—Healing: Restoring the Broken

1. Luke 4:18
2. 2 Corinthians 1:4
3. Proverbs 18:13 NIV
4. Proverbs 20:6
5. C. S. Lewis, *The Problem of Pain* (New York: HarperOne, 2001), 93.
6. James O. Prochaska, John Norcross, Carlo Diclemente, *Changing for Good* (New York: Avon Books, 1994).

Chapter 6—Letting Go: Accepting What Is

1. Ecclesiastes 3:1–8
2. Matthew 23:37
3. 1 Peter 3:18 NASB
4. 1 Peter 5:7

Chapter 7—Romancing: The Attraction Factor
1. Song of Songs 1:1
2. Proverbs 30:18–19 NIV
3. 1 Corinthians 7:5

Chapter 8—Putting It All Together
1. John 15:16
2. 1 Corinthians 13:13

A Final Thought
1. 1 John 4:8
2. James 2:8; emphasis added

ABOUT THE AUTHOR

Dr. John Townsend is a psychologist, entertaining speaker, and the bestselling author and coauthor of numerous books, including the Gold Medallion Award-winning *Boundaries* and *God Will Make a Way*. He is cohost of the nationally syndicated *New Life Live!* daily radio program and cofounder of the Cloud-Townsend Resources in Southern California. He holds a doctoral degree in clinical psychology from Rosemead Graduate School of Psychology at Biola University.